MORE
LIVES
THAN
A CAT

MORE LIVES THAN A CAT

GOLDIE DOWN

Southern Publishing Association, Nashville, Tennessee

Copyright © 1979 by
Southern Publishing Association

This book was
Edited by Don Short
Designed by Mark O'Connor
Cover painting by Ronald Hester

Type set: 10/12 Melior
Printed in U.S.A.

Library of Congress Cataloging in Publication Data

Down, Goldie M
  More lives than a cat.

    1. Turner, Thomas Trussler, 1927-   2. Seventh-day Adventists—South
Africa—Biography. 3. Clergy—South Africa—Biography.   I. Title.
BX6193.T87D68   286'.73 [B]   79-17814
ISBN 0-8127-0243-3

CONTENTS

PART ONE

Those Terrible Turner Kids

Young Tom Turner's activities attracted trouble as surely as a magnet attracts iron. When he was only a blue-eyed, flaxen-haired cherub, scarcely out of diapers, he and his brother George tried to nail a playmate's head to the floor.

It happened one rainy morning when Mrs. Turner was upstairs making beds, leaving her three children and the neighbor's boy playing happily in front of the living-room fire.

Rosy-cheeked Tom soon became bored with his windup cars and wandered around the house looking for something more exciting to do. On the kitchen stool he spied a hammer and a tin of nails forgotten by his father. Seized with a sudden desire to drive a nail into something, Tom grasped the hammer in his chubby hands and looked around.

Little Ronnie Landers—from across the street—sat on the floor, piling building blocks one upon another for baby Joan to knock over. Their squeals of delight changed to apprehensive howls when Tom advanced with his hammer and nail.

George looked up and caught onto the idea immediately. He downed Ronnie with a flying tackle and tried to hold his head still while Tom drove the nail home.

But Ronnie struggled and fought and bit. Joanie shrieked, and the brothers shouted. The commotion brought Mrs. Turner running from the bedroom.

"Stop it!" she yelled down the stairs. "Tom, George, stop it!"

She had no idea what her sons were doing, but past experience and present uproar dictated that whatever it was, they should stop it immediately.

Tom and George, though not noted for their obedience, desisted long enough for Ronnie to escape, and tragedy was averted.

Tom's birth certificate states that he came into the world at Liphook in Hampshire, England, on March 11, 1927, and that he was named Thomas Trussler Turner. It does not state what time of day or night he arrived, or whether it was hot or cold, wet or fine. Old England is usually cold and blustery at that time of year, so it is not likely he received a warm welcome weatherwise.

His welcome familywise is uncertain too. With his brother George only thirteen months old, Mrs. Turner was not especially happy at having another baby so soon—particularly not another boy. In those days parents set much store in having a "pigeon pair," a boy first and then a girl. But she got her girl soon enough. Tom was only thirteen months old when a sister, Joan, arrived.

Mr. Turner was a sergeant major in the Royal Engineers at Longmoor Camp, a few miles out of Liphook. He was away from home a lot, and poor Mrs. Turner nearly ran her feet off keeping house and caring for three little ones.

The Turner house, with its tablecloth-sized yard, lingered beside a dirt road on the outskirts of Liphook. Traffic seldom ventured into this dead end, and the children from the dozen nearby houses regarded the road as their playground, which partly accounts for the fact that when Tom was four and a bit he was hit by a truck.

It happened too long ago now to try and work out who was at fault. It is sufficient to state that when the truck careered around the corner and the other youngsters scattered, Tom did not make it. The front fender caught his head and tossed him into the ditch. For a moment he lay stunned, and his playmates thought he was dead. But then he stirred, sniveled, and raised his voice so lustily that every woman within earshot came at a run.

Those Terrible Turner Kids

The truck driver raised his voice too. Whether in apology or explanation is not certain, because he did not have a chance of being heard once Tom put his hand to his head and discovered blood.

Blood! His bellows intensified. His mother gathered him up and rushed him into the house, followed by all the women and kids and the truck driver—everyone giving advice; all talking at once; no one listening to anyone else.

Mother sat him on the kitchen table. Some woman had the good sense to pop a toffee into his bawling mouth, and that took care of the noise while his physical condition was assessed. He was not dead; that was certain. His bones appeared to be intact. Mrs. Landers fetched warm water and bathed his bloodied brow. Mother brought one of Dad's clean white handkerchiefs and pressed it hard against the wound to stanch the bleeding. But the women all agreed that the gash was too deep and wide for home treatment, so Tom must be taken to the doctor.

While Mrs. Turner scurried into the bedroom to change into her "going-out" dress, Mrs. Landers and another woman scrubbed Tom's hands and knees and forced his reluctant torso into clean clothes. Then off they went, with Tom still holding the handkerchief pressed tightly to his forehead and feeling extremely important. But the show was over. The children had returned to their play and the women to their housework, and to Tom's great disappointment hardly anyone noticed their going.

Dr. Gosling, the Turner family doctor, also belonged to a great many other families too, and a lot of people waited ahead of Tom and his mother. It seemed hours that Tom sat in the dim waiting room examining the worn carpet, with the red and yellow roses on it, and the green glass vase of paper flowers on the wall—he never did puzzle out what kept it there—and the gateleg table with a few yellowed copies of Punch. Tom knew they were Punch because he heard one of the older children say so.

At last Tom's turn came. By then his forehead was stiff and

9

cold, and the doctor gave him an injection to deaden the pain while he stitched the wound. Tom bellowed some more, and his mother promised him the earth, if he'd only shut up and keep still. The cuts were bad, and the scars they left above his eyebrows were there for life.

The accident slowed Tom down for a short time, but it did not knock any sense into his young head. He was soon back into his old form, whooping and hopping and trying to be in every place at once and making enough noise for ten little boys his size.

Before his wounds were properly healed, leapfrog became the rage. Leapfrog is a fine game if it is played correctly, but with no adult supervision, the street game usually got out of hand, and on this particular day it was bedlam. Children, big and little, ran around in circles, running and leaping and bending in joyous abandon. Young Tom Turner pivoted in the thick of it, running the fastest and shouting the loudest, until someone jostled him, and he fell heavily, doubling his leg backward.

What a hullabaloo he raised! Mother Turner came running out and carried him off to Dr. Gosling again, but this was something the good doctor could not handle in his office. He wrote an order and sent them on, by bus, to Haslemere Hospital.

There they found that Tom had a greenstick fracture. The doctor in emergency bound his leg in plaster and admitted him to the hospital for the night. The frightening array of white cots—some with weird frames holding rope and pulley attachments—and the wide variety of plaster casts displayed in the fracture ward struck terror into his small soul. Now there was no mother or George or Joanie to reassure him— only a lot of strange women marching up and down in crackly white aprons, telling him to lie still and be good, and bringing him a dish of bread and milk and an orange for supper.

A very much subdued boy was transported home on the carrier of his father's bicycle the next day. For a week or two Tom's "wooden leg" curtailed his outdoor activities and nearly drove his mother berserk trying to keep him amused indoors. But soon he was dashing around on two legs again, as irrepressible as ever.

George was six years old and Tom was five when Mother walked out of their lives. They came home from school one afternoon and found that she was gone. She left Joan with Mrs. Landers and disappeared—just like that. Perhaps she left a note for Father, but the boys were too young to know anything about that. Nor did they understand the reason for all the whispering among the neighbors whenever someone mentioned Mother's name.

After an initial day or two of staying with Mrs. Landers and howling and whimpering for Mamma, Tom settled down and accepted things as they were.

Aunt Julie, Mother's older sister, came down from London and took Joan to live with her. Dad Turner took the boys back home and cared for them as best he could.

It must have been twelve years later, when Tom was old enough to "breast the bar" and down a mug of beer with the best of them, that he and his dad were leaning their elbows on the bar of the local pub. Dad was not drunk, but he had reached the stage of maudlin confidences, and he hinted to his son that Mother had left home because she was fond of other men's company. Dad sighed deeply and blew the froth off his mug with an air of deep sadness.

Aunt Julie blamed Mother too. "Your mother loved flirting," she told the trio one day, thinning her lips disapprovingly. They did not reply. One didn't argue with Aunt Julie; but by then Tom was old enough to know that there are two sides to everything, and Mother might not have wandered had she received more consideration from Dad.

Dad Turner arranged with his superiors at Longmoor to have as much free time as possible. At least he must be home at night to get the boys' supper and see them to bed. They were supposed to be in school all day and to go to a neighbor's house in the afternoons when school let out, but they seldom did either. George and Tom became master in the art of playing hooky and getting into all kinds of mischief.

When word reached Mr. Turner's ears that his young sons were running wild through the village, he tried renting half his house to Mr. and Mrs. Saunders with the understanding that they keep an eye on the boys when he was in camp. But that did not work out. The Saunderses, an older couple, vastly overrated the innocence of childhood and underrated the devilish ideas those wide-eyed Turner boys hatched in their small heads. They saw them off to school each day with books and lunches and suitable admonitions; but when evening came the Saunderses were extremely gullible about the day's doings.

Fibbing came to Tom as naturally as breathing, and he never ran short of plausible explanations for the state of their clothes or late arrival home.

Mr. and Mrs. White were another fine old couple who had a soft spot for motherless boys. They were friends of Dad Turner's and owned a small saloon named the Deer's Hut, about a mile out of Liphook. Tom and George knew they could march into the bar at any time and be sure of a glass of barley water and a handful of cookies.

But on days that the pair played hooky they carefully avoided the Deer's Hut, although it lay on the direct route to their favorite haunt. They slunk along behind the back fence, hoping that Mrs. White would not come outside to hang clothes on the line or empty the tea leaves onto her garden.

Once safely past the pub they detoured through the fields and out into the ferny glens and groves of the downs. Thrilling with excitement, they crept like conspirators through the emerald grass, heavy dew soaking their shoes and socks and great, cold drops spattering them from overhanging trees. They spoke in whispers and held their breath in horror if one of them cracked a twig or dislodged a clattering stone.

On many a day when they should have been in school the pair roamed the downs, exploring every shady nook and clump of bushes. In sunny spring they pretended to be brave explorers, pushing their way through a jungle of prickly bushes in search of treasure in the form of half-ripe berries that made their tongues pucker.

On sullen wintry days they sloshed through muddy fields, light rain misting their caps and woolen sweaters. Sometimes they disturbed a hare and watched it dash off, its wet fur plastered to its sinewy body. Then they fancied themselves as hunters and bang-banged their stick guns at anything that moved.

By the time they could read well, pirate stories caught their imagination, and they scouted around for a suitable place to dig a pirate cave.

"This ought to do." Tom pointed to a small hillock where part of the earth had sheared away, disclosing a tangle of intertwining grass roots.

"Good O." George grabbed a stick and sent the first dirt flying. Tom joined him, and they puffed and pawed and dug into the sandy bank, shoving the dirt behind them as they went, working with the tireless energy they reserved for all unnecessary tasks.

It took days of playing hooky to finish the tunnel. Not consecutive days—Tom and George were too cunning for that. But a day away from school now and then was not questioned too closely. Probably the poor, harassed teacher was not sorry to have "those terrible Turner kids" out of his schoolroom as often as was decently possible without having to make inquiries.

As soon as the tunnel was long enough the boys took it in turns to worm their way in and begin the larger job of widening it out to make a cave. They wanted to have it big enough so that they could sit up straight and even crawl around a little.

It was pitch dark, and they dug blindly, like a pair of moles. It smelled damp and earthy—and was alarmingly dangerous. But the brothers, blissfully ignorant of that, reveled in the secrecy of their hideout.

Years later Tom revisited Liphook and made a sentimental pilgrimage to the downs where George and he had so often played. The tunnel they so laboriously dug had long since washed away, but the cave was still there. He shuddered to think what could have happened if the loose soil had caved in as they dug. No one would ever have known what happened to them.

On the opposite side of town from the Deer's Hut, old Mr. Powell had a cottage and garden, with a few pens of fowls. Mrs. Powell was dead, and the old man lived there alone. He did not seem to mind the Turner boys hanging around his place weekends or after school when they had nothing else to do. He did not yell at them and drive them away as some of the neighbors did. Perhaps in his rough sort of way he felt sorry for the pair of motherless waifs and thought that they were better off puttering about with him, where at least someone kept an eye on their doings. He let them follow him around and watch as he mixed up mash and fed his fowls and changed their water and collected eggs.

They watched him nail up the torn pens after foxes pawed the wire and tried to get inside. He kept a gun to deal with "them varmints," and they knew the drawer in the old dresser leaning against the wall of the tumbledown shed where he kept the cartridges.

Tom used to shiver when the old man told them how he heard the fowls squawking during the night and crept out and fired at the bushy-tailed marauder that disturbed them. It sounded terribly exciting, and he felt sorry that Mr. Powell had "missed agin" and had no furry corpse to show them. Tom had no conception of death. Apart from a rare sparrow lying on the downs, he had never seen anything dead, and the idea of life having an end never entered his mind. Perhaps that accounted for the brothers' next major mischief.

One Sunday afternoon George and Tom wandered down to Mr. Powell's shabby cottage and found that he was not at home. They stared at each other, unable to believe their good luck. As quiet as a pair of shadows they crept around the back of the house to make sure that he was not working anywhere in his garden. There was no sign of his bent old back half-hidden in the rows of beans and corn, and he was

14

not down at the fowl pens.

Without a word passing between them, as one boy they made for the shed. The rickety door was secured by a piece of twisted wire, but that proved no obstacle to eager fingers. Scarcely daring to breath, the two tiptoed inside and looked up at the right-hand wall, where the old gun was kept.

"He hasn't taken it with him," George breathed.

Supported by a couple of rusty nails, the gun lay snug against the old boards, well out of reach of curious small boys—but not determined ones.

"What can we stand on?" Tom looked around the shed, but there was no ladder, no boxes or broken chairs. Over in one corner he spied a pile of sturdy clay flowerpots, covered with dried mud and cobwebs. His eye lit up. He motioned to George, and both boys dashed over and dragged a big pot and a smaller one from the pile.

The pots were heavy and awkward to carry, but after much puffing and panting, they were in place directly under the gun, and the small pot was upside down on the larger one. Tom leaned against them, bracing them with his body while George climbed on.

It was a precarious perch and not quite high enough. By straining his utmost, George barely touched the gun with his fingertips. Again and again he tried, levering the weapon imperceptibly forward, so that at last it fell off the nail. Boys, gun, and flowerpots all landed on the cluttered floor together.

Without waiting to see whether the flowerpots were broken, Tom dived for the drawer of cartridges and stuffed a handful into his pocket. Then the pair of them scuttled outside and around the back of the old shed as if all the demons in hell were after them.

Neither George nor Tom had ever handled a gun before, but they had watched old Mr. Powell so many times that they knew just what to do. In no time the old gun was loaded, and they looked around for something to shoot at. They tried trees; that was easy. Too easy. There were no tins or bottles lying around that they could set up as targets. Then their eyes

15

lighted on the fowls. The obvious answer, and moving targets at that.

Totally oblivious to everything but the excitement of the moment, they took turns loading the gun and firing. Between them they had picked off a half dozen chickens, and Tom was in the act of aiming the gun again, when Mr. Powell charged around the back of the shed, waving his fists and shouting, "You young varmints! You so-and-so young varmints!"

Tom dropped the gun and fled. With George right behind him, he crashed through the tangled shrubbery and accumulated rubbish of years. Scratching his bare legs on exposed lumber, catching his sweater on blackberry thorns, he did not pause for breath until he was well away from Mr. Powell's backyard. Then the pair threw themselves down, panting and sweating, into the long grass that bordered the Anglican graveyard. Mr. Powell would never find them there.

For what seemed like hours the brothers hid in the long grass, flinching at every sudden sound, not daring to speak above a whisper. In fact, Tom did not feel like talking at all. He was too shocked and upset by Mr. Powell's reaction and the hurt that his words inflicted. Varmints, Mr. Powell had called them! Same as the despised foxes that stole his fowls. So he really did not like them at all. They were not "poor, motherless young'uns." They were varmints, undesirables.

Tom brooded over the revelation until his empty stomach told him that it was supper time. On the way home the brothers concocted a plausible tale to account for their long absence, and that was the end of the matter. Mr. Powell did not tell on them or demand reimbursement for his dead poultry. The only punishment they received was the one they inflicted on themselves by never going near his house again.

Next morning Tom discovered that he still had three of the cartridges in his trouser pocket. What could he do with them? He didn't know anyone else who owned a gun, and he couldn't hope to "borrow" Mr. Powell's gun anymore. Should he try somehow to sneak them back to Mr. Powell's shed? He told George about the cartridges, and for a couple of days they pondered the problem. Then George had a bright idea.

He sidled up to Tom on the school playground and whispered, "I wonder what would happen if we threw those cartridges into a fire."

Tom shook his head. He didn't know—but there was one sure way of finding out. Straight after school the pair raced home, snitched a box of matches from the kitchen, and ran almost the whole two miles to their hiding place on the downs.

George scraped a little hollow in the earth behind a clump of sheltering trees, and Tom dropped the cartridges in it, covering them with dead grass. Then they scurried around collecting dried leaves and twigs and piling them on top of the grass. When they had a sizable mound, George struck a match, and the leaves and grass burst into flame. It burned fiercly for a moment and then died without the twigs catching fire.

They gathered more grass and leaves. Again and again they tried, growing angrier every time the damp twigs failed to burn.

"Oh, dash it!" George threw the empty matchbox into the nearest bush and stamped off.

Tom looked for a stick and poked around in the little pile of ashes, trying to retrieve the cartridges, but they were too hot to handle, and he reluctantly followed his brother homeward.

The smell of smoke about their clothes and hair aroused Mr. Turner's suspicion, and when he finally wormed the story of that exploit out of the incorrigible pair, he decided that he'd had enough. He really couldn't cope, and his sons had better be put away before they killed themselves or somebody else.

PART TWO

Orphan Number 22

Tom was eight years old when Mr. Turner decided to send his sons to Dean Orphanage in Edinburgh. It was a natural choice because he was a Scot, and his parents lived in Portobello, a seaside resort not far from Edinburgh.

It seemed to Tom that Father had no sooner told them of his decision than their belongings were packed, their tickets purchased, and they'd said good-bye to the Whites and Landers.

The excitement of the long bus journey was eclipsed by the dread of the unknown, and while they waited at the depot, George and Tom tried to hide their fears by being more obstreperous than usual. They jostled each other, shouted, and plagued Dad with silly questions, and as soon as the bus pulled in, George flung himself into the seat, shouting, "I want the window seat."

"Not fair," Tom whined, rushing after him and trying to drag him off the seat. "You always have the window."

"Liar!" George punched wildly in Tom's direction. "How could I? We've hardly ever been on a bus before."

Red to the ears, Mr. Turner grabbed them by their collars and pulled them apart. They still glared at each other and yelled accusations, and the dispute might never have been settled if a tactful old lady sitting behind them had not declared that she didn't care so much about a window seat and Tom was welcome to have hers if only he'd stop yelling.

The first time the "lolly boy" came through the bus, Mr. Turner wisely armed himself with packets of sweets and

18

chewing gum and kept his sons' mouths full. Their eyes and hands were occupied with the piles of comics he thrust onto their laps, so that, apart from surreptitious kicks at each other under the seat, the boys maintained a fairly peaceful truce for the duration of the journey.

Edinburgh's weak sunshine did little to dispel the cold, and Mr. Turner hustled his sons into a cab for the ride to Dean. With their destination so close, George and Tom sat as quiet as mice. Tom's apprehension mounted with each turn of the wheels. He scarcely knew what an orphanage meant. Apart from the fact that Dad said there would be a lot of other boys and girls there, he did not know what to expect.

His first glimpse of Dean Orphanage reminded Tom of his school history book. Through the great iron gates he saw lawns and gardens as spacious as a city park and over to one side what looked like an old stone castle with towers at either end.

The taxi drew up in front of the gates, and Tom tumbled out and walked with George and Dad along a gravel path leading up to a massive front door. His knees knocked when Dad pulled the bell and he heard the far-off echo of its ringing, and he wished with all his might that he was back home in Liphook.

A maid answered the doorbell and ushered them into the governor's office. Tom had a vague impression of tall bookcases and cupboards with giant locks and in the center of the room a huge desk piled with papers and someone wearing a tweed coat seated behind the desk. The maid said, "Mr. Turner and his sons, sir," and she went out.

"Sir" in the shapeless tweed coat stood up and leaned over the desk, extending a huge paw of a hand to Dad and booming: "Well, well, Mr. Turner. How do you do?"

Mr. Turner shook hands and murmured something in reply, and they all sat down. Tom's legs trembled so hard that he could not have stood much longer anyway. Never had he seen such a colossal man. He towered over Dad, and Dad was no runt. To Tom's childish eyes the man behind the desk seemed to be about nine feet tall and nearly as wide. He had short, gray hair, and his ruddy face was unwrinkled, but all the same Tom was sure that he must be as old as Grandfather Turner, and *he* was past sixty.

But it was his eyes that held Tom like a magnet. Steely blue eyes that bored right through him. Tom fidgeted and hoped the man couldn't read his thoughts. He might not like it if he knew that Tom was thinking how much he resembled the terrifying giant in "Jack and the Beanstalk."

While Mr. Turner filled in a lot of papers, the governor leaned back in his chair, puffing his pipe and staring first at George and then at Tom. He asked their names, and George croaked a repy, but since Tom was too petrified to answer, Mr. Turner had to stop writing and introduce him.

The boys were tough little guys, certainly not the type to cry and cling to their dad and suffer from homesickness. All the same, Tom felt something besides chewing gum sticking in his throat as Dad's pen scratched away, and he realized that soon they would be left alone with that ogre sitting at the desk.

When Mr. Turner finished the papers and handed them over, there was quite a bit of conversation between him and the governor. As they made the final arrangements, Tom perched awkwardly on his high-backed chair, cowering under the glassy gaze of austere gentlemen in high, stiff collars, staring down from rows of framed prints on the wall.

Then Mr. Turner counted out some money and pushed it across the desk, and he and the governor stood up and shook hands again, and the governor boomed: "Rest assured we'll take good care of them, Mr. Turner. That we will."

And Dad said, "Well, be good boys." He gave them each a quick pat on the head and hurried out.

The governor opened a side door and bellowed something Tom could not distinguish, and presently two older boys appeared and were told to take George and Tom and their boxes up to the dormitory.

In silence they climbed the stone stairs to the second floor.

The dormitories proved to be long rooms with rows of beds and closets, and small-paned curtainless windows. As soon as their boxes were deposited beside their assigned beds, the big boys left, and boys about their own ages—all sizes and shapes of them—seemed to materialize from the floor. They crowded around, eager to look George and Tom over and tell them about their new home.

"You have to work here," a red-haired boy, with more freckles than Tom had ever seen on one face, assured them. "You have to make your own bed every morning and keep your closet tidy and help on Saturdays. Everyone does, except the babies." A slightly contempuous term, Tom learned, for the preschoolers who were under the care of Hetty, herself an orphan raised at Dean.

"The maids do the washing and the cooking." A boy with buckteeth took up the tale. "But Miss Beatty makes the girls help them."

"Who's Miss Beatty?" George asked.

"She's the matron," the crowd chorused. A skinny lad with a squeaky voice explained that Miss Beatty took care of the girls, who were in dormitories in the wing at the opposite end of the building. He warned them that it was strictly out-of-bounds, and woe betide any boy of any age who was caught lingering in those forbidden precincts. That piece of information led to a discussion about the rules at the home and how the governor enforced them. And that led to a discussion of the governor himself.

There were lots of stories about Robert Moffat David Barnes, the governor of Dean Orphanage. And it seemed that each batch of new arrivals was frightened into trembling submission by the other boys' stories about his terrible temper, his heavy hand, and his ability to read a boy's mind.

"He was a sergeant or a general or something, in the army, before he retired," volunteered a sniffly small boy, who smelled of eucalyptus and camphorated oil. "He's awfully smart, though. No one can put anything over him. Hettie says he sees everything because he's got eyes in the

21

back of his head."

Tom had never heard that expression before. He dimly realized that it must be a figure of speech—no one could *really* have eyes in the back of his head. All the same a mental image of that great giant of a man, equipped with four eyes so that he saw everything that went on, remained with him, and it was only with difficulty that he brought his attention back to what the others were saying. Their red-haired chief informant and another boy were arguing.

"That's not true," the ginger-head said. "He doesn't hit us for every little thing at all. Mostly he pretends not to notice our pranks."

"Yes, but when we . . ."

As he listened to them stating their cases with all the eloquence of budding lawyers, a gleam of hope pierced Tom's gloom. He concluded from the evidence given that the governor ignored harmless mischief but was always one jump ahead when real trouble was afoot.

"Have you heard about his wife?" asked a skinny lad with thick spectacles and a sagging lower lip.

George and Tom shook their heads, and silence fell on the whole group. Almost as if a signal had been given, those boys who were not already sprawled on beds or floor joined those who were. Sensing that this must be a tale of much import and it was better to be seated for the hearing of it, George and Tom balanced uncomfortably on their boxes and looked expectantly at the skinny lad. He remained standing, obviously enjoying being the focus of attention.

The skinny boy blinked a few times, cleared his throat like a true public speaker, and began. "Some time before I came here, Mrs. Barnes took sick. She was terribly ill, and finally she died." On the last word his voice sank to a husky, sepulchral tone, and his sagging lip drooped even lower.

"They put her in a coffin and screwed the lid down and waited all morning while a big hole was dug in the graveyard. People sent flowers, and a lot of them came to pay their last respects. My granny came, and that's how I know about it.

When everything was ready, everyone went to the graveyard for the burial. Just before they lowered the coffin into the hole, someone standing close to it said he heard a tapping——"

The skinny boy paused, and Tom felt the hair rising on the back of his neck. He could not tear his fascinated eyes from the boy's face. His breath came in short quick gasps as he willed the boy to finish the story.

"They unscrewed the lid and took it off, and sure enough, Mrs. Barnes was alive. They took her out of the coffin and brought her home, and she's still living downstairs, in the apartment right under our dorm." With a fine sense of drama, he ended his tale by rolling his eyes and pointing to the floor.

Tom could not speak or move for the horror that gripped him. A lot of the other boys seemed to be affected too, for the group broke up after that and left George and Tom alone to unpack their belongings and put them into their closets.

Weeks later Tom saw Mrs. Barnes. She was a thin little wisp of a woman who inspired him with dread each time their paths crossed. He had nothing against her, but he was almost relieved when eventually she died for good, and the governor married Miss Beatty, but that was well in the future.

It was hair-raising tales like that of Mrs. Barnes's resurrection that affected Tom's young mind. Tough as he was, terror filled him whenever he went near a graveyard. Right outside the east portion of the high wall surrounding the orphanage there was a cemetery, and Tom shivered whenever he had occasion to pass it. How many people under those gravestones had been buried alive as Mrs. Barnes nearly was? Did ghosts really dance on the tombstones at midnight as some of the boys vowed they did? Saggy-lip said he knew someone who had actually SEEN them. Did dead people come back and haunt the living?

Sometimes Tom lay awake at night trembling, imagining all sorts of fearful visitations from ghouls and ghosts. Or worse still, he slept and had nightmares of iridescent skeletons reaching for him with outstretched bony arms. Then Tom woke up screaming, and George, in the next bed, asked if he was sick—and if not, then he'd better shut up, or the monitor would be in to see what was wrong.

Life soon settled into a routine. Mondays to Fridays the children went to school in Dean village about a mile away from the orphanage.

Weekday mornings began with the agony of leaving their warm beds and struggling into school clothes. Edinburgh is always cold—only in winter it is colder than summer. First one to the bathroom got the hottest water, so every morning there was a mad scramble, with boys pushing and jostling and the timid ones lagging behind and having to splash their faces with a few drops of icy water. For the first few days, that was George and Tom, but it did not take them long before they shouted and jostled along with the rest.

Next came the mad rush to make beds. They had to be made properly too. None of this pulling the blankets up and trying to make them look smooth over rumpled sheets. No, the boys had to make sure the creases were out before the bedspread went on; otherwise they were sent upstairs to do them all over again. With the beds made they were free to clatter down and take their places in the first-floor dining room.

Girls and boys breakfasted together in the great dining hall with Matron Beatty in charge. She allowed no nonsense either. They all sat up, ate up, and shut up. As soon as they finished breakfast, the children lined up for inspection, which was carried out with military precision to the count of one, two, three.

Miss Beatty had two fat chins and an imposing bosom. Her eyes were as steely blue and her stern gaze as coldly quelling as the governor's. Tom dreaded to incur her displeasure and waited in trepidation when she approached.

"One!" All the children stood at attention, and she looked them over front view.

"Two!" They all smartly about-faced so that she had a back view and could check whether their hair was combed and their collars turned down and the heels of their shoes polished.

"Three!" Every child bent over so that Miss Beatty could see whether there were any holes in the boys' trousers or whether the girls had skirt hems hanging. If she found anything amiss, she ordered the culprit upstairs to change or hustled him off to the sewing room for instant repairs.

Inspection over, Miss Beatty said, "All right, you may go," and two hundred or more children thankfully scurried off to collect their school books from the study room and their sack lunches from the kitchen before dashing out the gate. Shepherded by officious prefects (monitors), the laughing, sulking, running, dawdling group reached the foot of the hill, where they parted company. The younger boys and girls went to the local primary school, and the older ones to various high schools.

George and Tom attended school in Edinburgh with about as much enthusiasm as they had in Liphook, the only difference being that here they had less opportunity for playing truant. These teachers kept a close watch on their charges, besides being handy with a cane themselves, and the boys knew that any serious misdemeanor would be reported to the governor. That in itself was sufficient deterrent for stouter hearts than theirs.

Neither George or Tom were bright pupils. They were not dull either. Scholastically they managed to keep about the middle of the class. But in their minds, lessons were something that had to be endured in between recess and lunch break when they could play. The older boys played team games, but younger ones like Tom tore around the playground in their own wild versions of hide-and-seek and tag that often ended with bloodied noses and skinned knees and elbows.

One recess they raced around like a nest of stirred ants, chasing first one and then another; grabbing wildly at flying ties and shirttails; dashing in and out around the toilet block; skidding on the loose gravel; shouting; sweating. Tom tore around the corner of the building yelling, "Can't catch me!" at the top of his voice and ran full pelt into a boy coming from the opposite direction. Their heads met with a resounding WHAM.

Dizzy, and half-blinded by the blow, Tom staggered drunkenly, and before he recovered his balance the boy rushed up and hammered him with clenched fists. "Why don't you look where you're going?" he shouted.

Tom hardly felt the boy's indignant blows for the agonizing pain in his eye and for his throbbing temple. Even though an exploratory hand revealed no blood, he was sure his forehead was dented.

Experience had taught Tom the futility of looking to anyone in authority for help or sympathy; so he bore the pain in sniveling silence, but it was weeks before his head ceased aching, and his left eye remained permanently injured.

In the afternoons when the orphanage children arrived home from school they dumped their books, changed their clothes, and ran to the kitchen for something to eat. Cook always had a huge basket of bread and butter waiting, one slice for each child.

One afternoon Tom had after-school detention, and when he arrived at the kitchen door there was only one piece of bread left in the basket. A pig-tailed girl lingering nearby, noisily chewing the last of her piece, told him the other kids had rejected that slice because they said the orphanage cat had wet on it.

"Go 'n' fall on yer head!" Tom took a menacing step forward, and Pigtails shrieked and ran.

He poked the bread with a tentative finger, decided it felt a bit soggy and, barging into the kitchen's sacred precincts, asked for another slice of bread.

The cook, poor woman, was hardened to children's complaints and told him to eat it or get nothing. What's more, she stood over him to make sure he did.

Tom ate it, . . . and the awful taste lingered in his mouth for days.

At Dean Orphanage Saturdays were devoted to chores. Tom did not know what the girls did on their side of the great house—helped the cook or housemaids, maybe, or learned to sew or knit. Miss Beatty found plenty to keep them occupied, that was certain.

On the boys' side there were always great piles of wood to be chopped and stacked, mountains of coal to be carried, and the lawns to mow. Most of Dean's twenty acres was lawn, and they had no power mowers either. The smart governor devised a way of making the old-fashioned hand mowers into two-boy power by fastening a rope to the front so that one boy pulled while the other pushed.

Sometimes the boys squabbled and complained about their work, but usually they managed to make a game out of even the hardest chore. Every month the work roster rotated so that each boy had a change of job, sometimes hard work, sometimes easy.

If the children hurried, they had time for team sports on Saturday afternoons. Boys on one side of the spacious grounds and girls on the other, and the governor hovering like an avenging angel on the sidelines.

Even rainy Saturday afternoons were fun—for the children. The girls played parlor games, or table games, such as ludo, snakes and ladders, and others. The little ones had dolls and doll beds. All sorts of feminine activities kept them busy and happy.

But the boys ran wild in the veranda common room on the ground floor. The noise of a hundred or more assorted boys clomping in and out, banging doors, shouting and jostling, was calculated to jar the stoutest nervous system. The Barneses habitually endured the ruckus for an hour or so, probably realizing that trying to stop it would be akin to trying to block the tide with a pitchfork. Then the governor came to the top of the stairs and tossed down a half dozen new tennis balls.

"Hurrah! Hooray!" The boys cheered and yelled and

scrambled after the balls, and the one who was lucky enough to catch a ball kept it. By common consent he owned it. He wrote his name on it, and it was recognized as *his* ball, even though the rest of the boys played with it.

One rainy Saturday the cooped-up boys dashed around thumping and shouting, making more noise than necessary, hoping for the customary tennis balls. Sure enough, when the governor could stand no more, he stomped out to the landing above their heads, leaned over the railing, and bellowed, "Here, catch!"

The balls bounced in all directions, and joy of joys, one landed on Tom's head. Heart pounding with excitement, he grabbed it and hugged it to his chest. The possessor of a tennis ball of his own gained a sense of power. "It's my ball. You've got to let me have first throw.... I get to pick sides because it's my ball. . . . It's *mine*."

Tom's thrill of ownership was short-lived. Before he even had time to scrawl his name on the velvety, white surface, a bigger boy snatched the prize from his clutching hands and ran off with it.

Tom turned to chase the culprit, who disappeared among the writhing, wriggling mass of boy-bodies. The injustice of it was more than Tom could bear. Fury wiped out fear, and before he knew what he was doing, he bounded up the winding stone staircase and knocked on the governor's door.

"Sir," he blurted tearfully when the door opened and the governor's huge bulk towered over him. "Sir, he took my ball. I caught it first. It was mine. He——"

The governor's red face blazed under his white hair. "Get out!" he roared, slapping Tom across the face with a huge hand.

Transfixed by the shock of this further injustice, the boy stood staring at him. When he made no move, the governor leaned down, took him by the scruff of the neck and the seat of the pants, and booted him down the stairs.

Tom learned about life in the orphanage. That day he found out that often the strong triumph while the weak suffer and justice is not always meted out as it should be. But even in the midst of his tears, as he picked himself up at the foot of the stairs, he dimly realized that the governor's action was not in character. Mr. Barnes was a hard man, stern and harsh, but normally just and fair in his dealings with the boys. Perhaps the rain and their noise had goaded him beyond endurance that day, or perhaps he had been drinking too much.

For days Tom smarted from that injustice, but it never occurred to him to run away. He was happy at the orphanage. George was there with him, and though they sometimes quarreled with each other, they presented a united front against enemy attack.

But some of the other boys ran away. Particularly Tommy Coutts. He often ran away, was caught, brought back, and given "six of the best" from the governor. The boys felt sorry for Tommy and smuggled him a bit of old eraser to bite on so he could keep his dignity and not howl; but before the governor got through with his chastisement the bit of eraser flew to the floor, and Tommy was in full voice. Mr. Barnes was not an ex-boxer for nothing. He still had plenty of muscle and knew how to deal with recalcitrant boys.

At Dean Orphanage a public whipping was the most dire form of punishment. The whole household assembled in the great hall, and Miss Beatty and the governor stood up on the platform with the culprit looking very forlorn between them. The governor announced his crime and then boomed, "Bend over!" and raised his strap. He had an old leather strap that he kept for the purpose, and it was whispered among the boys that he heated the end of it in the fire so that the leather went dry and hard to make it hurt like fury.

As the culprit bent over, it seemed that all the other children caught their breath and watched in fascinated horror, chills of pity—or sympathy—running through them as the strap rose and fell.

When he finished, the governor folded his strap very deliberately, and while Miss Beatty led the sobbing culprit away, he looked silently around at the assemblage, his steely eyes saying as plain as words, "Now then, anyone else like to try any tricks?"

The quivering onlookers stood dumb as posts, and after one last glare over the whole group, the governor turned on his heel and left the platform. At a word from the monitors the children filed out, quiet and subdued, with none of the usual pushing and jostling.

At either end of the great house, wide stone staircases led down from the top floor in a series of turns like giant z's: down a dozen steps to a small landing, turn; down another dozen steps, another landing, and so on to ground level, where at the boys' end, the wood was kept neatly stacked in the stairwell. Except for rainy days the boys were forbidden to play in, on, or near the stairs or the stairwell, and the woodpile and its environs was out-of-bounds unless they happened to be working there stacking firewood.

Most of the boys obeyed the rules, but a few were of the type that when something was forbidden, that was the thing they most wanted to do. Tom fitted into that category, so one Saturday afternoon in winter, Ian Walker and he played in the forbidden area. They made a great game out of clambering over the pile of wood, rearranging the sticks, and reveling in the thrill of disobedience. Suddenly they heard the governor's apartment door open and his heavy footsteps above. Petrified, they listened to him walk along the veranda and start down the stairs.

Fear lent wings to Ian's feet. He scrambled down from his perch and fled to glorious safety. But the same emotion held Tom fastened to the spot. In any case, he was on top of the highest stack, and it was too late for him to run. He could never get down in time to escape without the governor's seeing him against the square of light that was the open doorway. Mr. Barnes knew every boy both by name and number, and there was no chance of his not being recognized.

Tom's heart pounded like a jackhammer. He pushed himself further back into the gloomy corner and screwed up as small as possible. He knew that if the governor looked up or shone his flashlight in that direction, he would be discovered, and what the punishment would be he shuddered to think.

Puffing from exertion, Mr. Barnes stooped to enter the dark little room, and Tom held his breath. The governor shone his flashlight from side to side, apparently looking for wood the right length. Then he bent over and filled his arms with firewood from a lower stack and slowly labored back up the stairs.

Tom dared not move until he heard the governor's door slam on the floor above, then heedless of splinters in hands and bottom, he slid down the woodpile and dashed out into the clean, pure air of freedom.

On Sundays the inhabitants of Dean Orphanage went to church. Everyone attended. Only the most excruciating toothache or the whoopiest cough was accepted as reason for missing kirk. They marched in a long crocodile formation, small children in front with Hettie and Miss Beatty, then the older girls, the older boys, and the governor bringing up the rear.

They filled the balcony of the old stone church. A cold, dim edifice with carved mausoleums of important people; stained glass windows; a hushed, almost tangible air of antiquity and solemnity. Not that the children were always solemn. Most of them, especially Tom, found it impossible to sit still and keep quiet for nearly two hours.

At the beginning of the service the hymns and prayers and responses provided diversion. Tom watched the choir stand up and sit down and shuffle their hymn sheets. He admired the way the organist manipulated all the keyboards of the great pipe organ. He thumbed through the prayer book and read a few words here and there. But by the time the sermon began, his attention span was growing shorter and shorter.

With the governor sitting not far away, Tom made valiant efforts to keep out of trouble by acquainting himself weekly with people in the stained-glass windows. Jesus was there, of course. It was easy to pick Him out because He had a circle of light around His head like one of Saturn's rings. In the pic-

tures of the child Jesus, the artist depicted Him holding a
white lily in one hand and a bird in the other. But in one of the
other windows, where He was grown up, He held a lamb over
his shoulder.

In the fourth window there were men crowding close to
Him, and Tom, supposing they must be the disciples, tried to
fit names to them. The one with the long white beard would
be Andrew or Peter. No, the one with the basket of fish might
be Andrew. The young one in red cloak, always so close to
Jesus, must be John. Mary, wearing a blue gown and having a
white shawl over her head, looked terribly, terribly sad. The
dark man with the sneering face must be Judas, and——

By that time Tom's legs would be prickling with pins and
needles, and he would have to wriggle or rub them to get the
circulation back. The monitor would glare at him, and he
would poke his tongue out at the monitor—behind his hand
so the monitor could not see him—and he would think, "It's
all right for YOU, you're nearly sixteen and your feet reach the
floor."

Tom's feet did not. At least not when he sat back in the
pew and leaned against the hard wooden backrest. Then they
stuck uncomfortably out in front of him. If he sat forward, near
the edge of the pew, his feet touched the floor and his back
slumped. Either way was torture for long periods. Year by
year Tom used to measure his growth by his feet's progress
toward the floor. At about age thirteen he felt it was a personal
triumph when he had a sudden spurt of growth and almost
overnight his back leaned comfortably against the seat-back
while the tips of his boots touched the floor.

Tom suspected that the governor did not enjoy church any
more than he did but that he felt it was his pious duty to
attend. When Mr. Barnes saw his charges becoming restless
during the sermon, about the time the minister said, "Now,
my second point is . . ." he would pass peppermints or yellow
and white striped humbugs along the rows and each child
popped one into his mouth.

It was considered the honorable thing to suck, not chew,

the candy. It lasted much longer; and besides, chewing made a jaw cracking, crunchy sound that was quite out of keeping with the reverent surrounding.

Tom never knew for sure whether it was the governor's peppermints or his eye-conveyed threats of a whipping that kept them all in order, but whichever it was, they usually managed to sit through church without any grievous misdemeanors, then crocodiled it back to the home for their Sunday dinner.

Probably it was the fact that the boys and girls from Dean Orphanage were gloriously free from adult supervision during their walk to and from school that made the exercise so enjoyable.

Of course there were a number of rules and regulations that had to be obeyed, and at all times they were expected to walk along decently and in order, with accompanying monitors to enforce laws and good conduct. But often enough the monitors were occupied with their own affairs: winking at the older girls; teasing one another in loud, newly acquired bass voices; and more or less ignoring the young fry as long as they were not doing anything too outrageous.

After school one afternoon, as Tom struggled Deanward with a couple of other eleven-nearly-twelve-year-olds, he became interested in a red delivery truck that preceded them along the street. He was intrigued with the way it stopped every little while and the driver dashed inside a shop to deliver some goods, lingering just long enough for the boys to catch up with the truck, and then driving off. Again and again the truck stopped, the driver hopped out and took a package of goods into the shop, the boys caught up with the truck, out came the driver, and off went the truck.

Suddenly Tom had a splendid idea. He took a quick look around to see whether there were monitors about, and without waiting for a second thought he thrust his bag of school books into a surprised mate's hand and ran behind the truck. A moment later the driver emerged from a shop and leaped into the truck cab, giving Tom scarcely enough time to jump for the tailgate and take a firm grip before the vehicle roared off.

The head-jerking suddeness of takeoff loosened Tom's hold and gave him no time to find a resting-place for his feet. He bent his knees and tried to keep his boots from dragging the road as it rushed past beneath him.

Before they had gone fifty yards, Tom knew that he had done the wrong thing. Hanging on to a moving vehicle was vastly different from hanging on gym bars. The strain nearly wrenched his arms out of their sockets. In spite of his desperate efforts to keep his knees bent, gravity pulled them downward, and they slowly straightened as the truck gathered speed. A final jolt and his feet bumped and dragged along the road.

Tom pressed his frantic face against the tailgate, and vibrations went through his head like a pneumatic drill. Dust filled his eyes and his yelling mouth. His teeth just about rattled out of his jaws.

"Stop! Stop!" he shrieked. Why wasn't the driver stopping at another shop? "Stop! Stop!"

But the driver could not hear above the noise of the engine, and Tom knew he would have to let go before his arms tore out of their sockets.

He closed his eyes to the terrifying sight of whirling dust and racing road, gritted his teeth, and prepared to drop. Just then the driver braked violently. Before the vehicle stopped, the driver leaped out and pounced on Tom.

"Yer flaming idiot boy! If that other motorist hadn't o' warned me!"

He jerked Tom off the truck, shaking him and boxing his ears with a violence that sent the boy sprawling into a huddle of market women gossiping on the curb.

"Yer orta have more sense at yor age!" The driver shouted and shook his fist. "Yer coulda been killed, yer could; and then I'd o' been up fer manslaughter."

Even as he scrambled to his feet Tom felt sure that it was

the latter thought that upset the driver most. The driver didn't care two hoots about Tom's fate, but the thought of the trouble that he would have been in if Tom had been hurt kept him glowering and raging.

Tom stood shaking and trying to make himself as small as possible while the driver ranted and raved at him. The shouting continued until the driver had circled the truck three times, assuring himself that no other "idiot boys" were clinging to the tailgate, before he climbed into the cab and roared off in a shower of gravel.

The kind women crowded about, brushing Tom's clothes down and assessing his injuries while they clucked over and over to each other, "He could have been killed! It's a wonder the boy wasn't killed!"

Red-faced with embarrassment, Tom struggled to escape their ministrations. As soon as they satisfied themselves that no bones were broken, they released their grip, and he scurried off and hid behind the nearest high fence to examine the damages for himself.

What a mess he was in! There was a button missing from his trousers, and his cap was gone. He hoped one of his mates saw it blow off and picked it up. His legs were scratched, and his hands stiff and burning. But it was his boots that worried him most. What would the governor say if he saw them? The leather toes were scuffed so badly that they would never be the same again.

Tom crouched behind the tall fence until his Deanmates passed and their voices died away in the distance, then he sneaked home the back way. While the others busied themselves with their bread and butter, he raced upstairs to the box where the shoe polish and brushes were kept and gave his boots the most thorough brushing they had ever had. There was no hope of restoring a shine to the worn toes, but he smeared black polish thickly on the scrapes and hoped that Miss Beatty would not notice.

For almost a week Tom trembled inwardly if the governor or Miss Beatty as much as looked in his direction, but apparently no one told on him; or if he did, Mr. Barnes chose to ignore the incident.

Tom's mates ribbed him in private, and he smarted under their teasing. It was a long, long while before he ceased to be indignant with the truck driver for choosing that moment to conclude the shop deliveries and subject him to such peril.

Bubble pipes were all the rage one year. Games and pastimes at Dean Orphanage used to go in and out of fashion like women's clothes. One year it was Yo-Yos. Everyone had a Yo-Yo, and one simply was not IN if he did not have, or could not borrow, a Yo-Yo. Next it was marbles, and boys and girls constantly wore the skin off their knuckles playing "bools" and "keeps" with their steelies and glassies. Then came spinning tops for boys and skipping ropes for the girls. Then everyone went back to ball games, and so the cycle went on.

This particular year it was bubble pipes, and nearly everyone had a white clay bubble pipe. All sorts of races and competitions were invented to see who could blow the biggest bubble or whose bubble lasted longest or whose floated highest before it burst. They looked pretty, too, those soap bubbles floating through the air, reflecting sunlight like spherical rainbows. Some of them wafted around for ever so long before bursting wtih a soft, sudsy pop.

But some of the lads found the clay pipes useful for something more sophisticated than blowing soap bubbles. On his way to school one morning Tom noticed a group of older boys lagging behind, heads bent, every now and again uttering small cries of triumph as they pounced to pick up something from the pavement.

Thoroughly intrigued, he lounged against a convenient post and waited for them to catch up. Sandy Webster was among them, as were Wally Gray and the Cooper twins from Dean, and Bob Somebody-or-Other and another fellow from the village.

"Wotcha doin'?" Tom asked when they were close enough.

"Aw, nick off, Tom." Sandy frowned at him and kept his hand in his pocket. "We don't want kids around."

"Kid yourself!" Tom retorted indignantly. "I'm nearly as old as you are."

"Maybe so," Sandy sneered. "But I'll bet you've never smoked."

That rocked Tom a bit, but he recovered quickly. "Bet I have too," he lied; and clear as day he knew what they had been up to—picking up cigarette butts off the street.

"Want to come with us then?" Wally was at least fourteen, and Tom, flattered by this invitation from an older boy, did not realize that by being clever enough to implicate him, Wally was thereby sealing Tom's lips.

"You'll have to find your own, though." Wally patted his pocket mysteriously. "We've only got enough for ourselves."

That was not hard. Tom took a different route home from school that afternoon, one that passed the local pub, and he easily picked up a handful of butts and a couple of half-smoked cigarettes.

The day the boys took their bubble pipes to school, the group of them spent the whole recess down at the farthest end of the playground, behind the toilet block, unraveling butts and shaking out the "precious" shreds of tobacco. Then they filled their clay pipes and, with trembling hands, applied the matches.

It took several days of recesses and a lot of patience before some of the boys got the hang of applying the match to the bowl of tobacco and drawing and puffing at just the right moment to ignite the weed. But finally they all got the knack of it and smoked, really smoked. Then they felt themselves to be at least twelve feet tall and absolutely grown up.

Tom was especially proud of his accomplishment, and every little while, in between long draws on his bubble pipe, he passed a surreptitious hand over his upper lip to feel whether he might have instantly acquired a downy growth to equal Wally's much-envied sign of budding manhood.

Of course they all went back into their classes smelling

like a tobacconist's shop, and the teachers did not need to be Sherlock Holmes to know what had been going on. They were immediately reported to the principal, who informed the governor, and when they arrived home from school one afternoon Mr. Barnes was waiting for them. He ushered Wally, Sandy, Tom, and the Cooper twins into his office.

They stood in a group in front of his huge desk while he leaned back in his chair, looking more ogrelike than ever, and growled, "So you think you're old enough to smoke, eh?"

His bushy white eyebrows drew together in a dreadful frown, and Tom's knees literally knocked together as he waited for sentence to be pronounced. The governor stared at them in a silence calculated to reduce the boldest boy to a state of terror and then said, "Well, you might as well learn to do it properly."

Tom relaxed a little and heard a faint sigh of relief from Wally, standing next to him. At least they were not going to be caned.

While the boys watched, the governor opened a desk drawer and drew out a handful of pipes—real briar pipes, shiny and almost new. He stuffed them into his bulging left-hand pocket, patted his right hand pocket for the reassuring rattle of a matchbox, and then stood up.

"All right, come along." he boomed, and marched them out of the building and across the wide expanse of lawn that led to the shrubbery on the girls' side of the orphanage.

Tom could not see any sign or hear any sound of feminine activity from the girls' rooms, but some extra sense told him that they were watching behind drawn curtains and giggling at the boys' discomfiture. Most of them knew what had been going on, and several of the older girls had predicted that they would be caught.

When the group reached the green seclusion of the shrubbery the governor lined them up facing him, handed each one a pipe, a plug of tobacco, and a knife. Then he said, "Now you watch me. I'll show you the proper way to smoke a pipe." He took out his own smelly briar and a worn pocketknife. "First you cut up your tobacco like this."

He held up his plug of tobacco—Mitchell's XXX Bogey Roll—vicious, black sticky stuff that stuck to their knives like glue. But with Mr. Barnes's eye upon them and his great hulk towering over them, the boys managed to hack off enough of the dreadful stuff to fill their pipe bowls.

"Right. Now tamp it down with your finger, like this. Tamp it well."

Following his every move, they tamped the tobacco tightly into their pipes, and then he handed each one a couple of matches.

"All right. Now light up. Keep watching me. Every time I draw, you draw. Every time I puff, you puff."

Striking the matches on the soles of their boots, the boys followed his instructions to the letter. Every time he drew on his pipe, they drew. When he puffed, they puffed.

But Mr. Barnes was an experienced smoker, probably been at it for fifty years, and they were only beginners. First one boy and then another turned pale green, threw up, and collapsed on the lawn, heaving and groaning.

Tom was the third to go. His nostrils felt parched and his head as big and heavy as a pumpkin, while his eyes stung and his tongue burned. The trees and bushes around the shrubbery rose and fell in time to the rhythm of his heaving stomach, until at last he staggered to the nearest flower bed and pulled the pipe from his mouth just in time.

The experience discouraged Wally's group for awhile, but it did not stop other boys from trying the same trick with cigarette butts and bubble pipes. It became a common sight to see the governor, his pockets bulging with briar pipes and tobacco plugs, marching little groups of boys across the girls' lawn to the shrubbery.

In 1939, not long after the smoking episode, World War II began, and the powers that be ordered the evacuation of children from the major cities. They expected Edinburgh to be one of the first cities bombed, so the children from Dean

Orphanage were sent to stay with kind people in the country. George and Tom Turner were billeted with Mrs. Mitchell at Tombrechachie in Glenlivet in the highlands of Banffshire.

Mrs. Mitchell's husband was dead, and her children all grown. The married girls lived with their husbands on nearby farms. Two unmarried sons, Bert and Jimmy, managed the home farm for their mother, so there was plenty of room for the Turner boys. Mrs. Mitchell was plump and kind and motherly, and George and Tom enjoyed the year they spent at her farm.

Several other city boys and girls were evacuated to Tombrechachie, and they all attended the small multigrade school where Mr. Hardy was master.

"Hardy by name and hard by nature," the local boys jeered behind his back, and young Tom joined in the jeering, though he secretly felt sorry for Mr. Hardy. Mr. Hardy limped when he walked, and Tom often speculated about how he came to have a lame leg. Was he born like that? Had he been in an accident? Maybe, like Dad, Mr. Hardy had fought in World War I and had been wounded. Whichever it was, Tom pitied the poor man.

There were thirty-two children in grades one to six crammed into that country schoolroom. It was a plain room with none of the bright paint and colorful wall charts and sets of illustrated encyclopedias that modern teachers consider so essential.

It had battered desks scored with generations of initials and inset with old-fashioned inkwells that formed the basis of many a prank. There was a large, tattered-at-the-edges world map rolled up on the wall above the blackboard. It had a rope and pulley arrangement so that when fifth and sixth classes studied geography, the map could be let down like a curtain over the blackboard. Mr. Hardy pointed out the continents and oceans with a long willow wand that doubled as a cane when necessary.

Many of the countries on the map were colored red or had red patches in them. This denoted that they were part of the

British Empire. Good old empire! Tom's skinny chest swelled with patriotic pride, and on the rare occasions that the school had a singing lesson—with songs suitable for the troubled times in which they lived—he yelled at the top of his voice, "Rule, Brittania! Britannia, rule the waves! Britons never shall be slaves!"

Besides the blackboard, which was cracked at the corners and was shiny in the middle so that the chalk slid over it with a shrill squeak that set Tom's teeth on edge, there were two small, faded prints on the walls.

One print showed Ruth clinging to Naomi and saying, "Intreat me not to leave thee," with Orpah, her face half-turned toward the hills of Moab, in the background. The words were printed underneath the picture, and every child in the school knew them by memory.

The other picture was of the boy David, slingshot in hand, running out to meet the huge, armor-clad giant, while in the distance the craven Israelites huddled about their tents, expecting to see Goliath cut him to shreds.

Nearly all the color had faded from the pictures, the glass was smeary, and the frames hung slightly crooked; but doubtless they had been put there to inspire the boys and girls to noble deeds. Certainly the one of David formed subject matter for many of Tom's daydreams. He pictured himself courageously slaying giants when he should have been wrestling with arithmetic problems.

In winter, snow lay thick on the ground at Tombrechachie, and during recess the children organized snow fights. They chose sides, and boys and girls all worked together building forts of packed snow and laying in arsenals of snowballs to fling at one another.

Mr. Hardy allowed the game as long as they threw balls of soft snow that shattered on impact and showered the enemy with a spray of glittering crystals, but if they put stones inside the snowballs or packed the snow in their hands until it became as hard as ice, they were in for trouble.

Once, when a fight was in full swing, one of the older boys

scooped up a big handful of snow and swung it around his head until it was solid, then threw with all his might in Tom's direction. Tom ducked and it whistled past him and hit one of the girls, making her cry and bringing Mr. Hardy limping to the door of the schoolroom.

"Turner, come here."

With hand already raised to return the throw, Tom protested his innocence. "It wasn't me, sir. I only——"

"I saw you," Mr. Hardy insisted. "I saw the snowball go from you to the girl." He reached for his willow cane.

The whacking he received for something he had not done did not improve Tom's relations with Mr. Hardy. From then on he successfully stifled any feelings of pity he had for the poor, harassed schoolmaster.

When the warm weather came George and Tom sometimes went out hunting with Mrs. Mitchell's sons or helped them a bit with the farm work; but there was not much that they could handle, and during the long summer vacation they became bored. That was when Malcolm came up with his diabolical idea.

Malcolm was a cockney evacuated from London and living with one of Mrs. Mitchell's sons-in-law. While school was out, he spent a lot of time over at the Mitchell farm playing with George and Tom. They did not realize it, but Malcolm was one of those boys who hatch up all kinds of mischief and egg others on to execute it, while they stand back and righteously keep out of trouble themselves.

It was Malcolm's idea that they make the clubs. On their own, George and Tom would probably not have done it, particularly with the long-ago shooting of Mr. Powell's chickens in the back of their minds. But with Malcolm urging them on, they each whittled a wooden club, the idea being that they throw it at a moving target and each time they scored a direct hit they carved a notch in the handle of their clubs.

At first they tried hitting birds. Scores of sparrows and pigeons frequented the yards and haystacks, but they were too quick for the boys. At first sign of movement they took wind and flew high into the air, well out of range. The farm dogs, lazily dozing in the sun by the barn, were easy prey; but they put up a terrible barking and howling when hit—beside they might retaliate. The chickens were just right.

It was Malcolm, of course, who pointed them out as ideal targets. The fowl yard was well away from the house, sheltered by trees that hid it from Mrs. Mitchell's view, and if anyone heard the fowls setting up an extra squawking and scuttling, they took no notice. Chickens are stupid creatures, always crowing or clucking about something.

As the weeks passed and the boys cut more and more notches in their club handles, poor Mrs. Mitchell became more and more puzzled over the injuries to her chickens. Some of the hens limped around scarcely able to keep themselves upright; others had mashed combs or swollen eyes. She simply could not understand and several times mentioned it at the dinner table. George and Tom felt uncomfortable and exchanged glances that meant they vowed off the sport. But a few days afterward, when they were wandering around the farmyard idle and bored, along came Malcolm, as insidious as Satan, and incited them on to fresh exploits.

"Go on," he urged. "No one knows it's you two, and you're getting real handy with that club, Tom. Score a bull's-eye nearly every time, you do."

Such admiration could not go unacknowledged, and soon the brothers would be at it again, cornering the poor fowls and flinging their wooden clubs at them.

Eventually they were caught. It is possible that Malcolm snitched on them. He was that kind of boy. Mrs. Mitchell did not order any corporal punishment for their cruelty, but the look of reproach and disappointment in her kind, tired eyes made them squirm like a pair of worms.

Only a matter of weeks later Mrs. Mitchell decided to move from the farm. George and Tom were sent back to Dean Orphanage for a month, then on to Musselburgh, to a small village called Cousland, where they lived with Mr. and Mrs.

Brown and their middle-aged son, Paddy.

Paddy was a coal miner—a great lump of a fellow with permanently grimy skin, bulging muscles, and an unshakable faith in the virgin Mary. Lying in their beds at night George and Tom could hear him through the thin wall, counting his beads and mumbling the Rosary in a deep, rumbling voice.

They were scared of Paddy. They were scared of Mrs. Brown too. She was a down-to-earth, forceful type of woman who would stand for no monkey business from any pair of gangly, towheaded teenagers. They boys really minded their p's and q's when she was around.

The nearest high school to Cousland was at Dalkeith. George and Tom had to leave early in the morning and trudge two miles along a country lane from the Brown's house to the main road, and another mile to the corner where they caught a bus into Dalkeith.

High school, for Tom, was a repeat of elementary school. He concentrated on learning as little as he possibly could. When the teacher was not looking he threw spitballs at the other boys. Occasionally he played hooky with George, and they spent the whole day lolling around in the soft meadow grass, smoking cigarettes stolen from Paddy, and talking— making grandiose plans for the future when they would be grown men and not have to do what anyone told them to do.

"I think I'll travel." Tom chewed the end of a grass stalk. "I'm sick of this cold country. I'd like to go someplace where it's warm. India maybe, or Australia."

"How'd you get there?" George scoffed. "Travel costs money, and you haven't got a bean."

Tom opened his mouth to argue, but the logic of his brother's statement made him shut it again. He rolled over and stuffed a handful of grass down the back of George's shirt.

George grabbed him by the hair and pushed his face into the dirt. And so they scuffled and talked and smoked and dreamed until the westering sun warned them that it was time to hurry back to the Brown's abode.

While they lived with the Browns, Tom learned to ride a bicycle. He had not had an opportunity before because at the orphanage the children walked everywhere they went; none of them had bicycles. There were no bicycles at the Mitchell's either. But Maggie, one of the girls who lived out Cousland way, rode a bicycle to school, and she was a little sweet on Tom and let him learn on hers.

At first Tom was awfully wobbly, zigzagged all over the road, and he fell off dozens of times. The other kids nearly killed themselves laughing at his efforts. Finally he got the hang of keeping his balance, and Maggie let him go off ahead on his own, provided he did not go very far and was very careful going down the big hill.

"Sure," he promised her with a blithe wave. "I'll be careful."

He was the picture of a sedate Sunday-afternoon cyclist as he started off, but as soon as he was out of Maggie's sight, he started to pedal faster and faster. He pumped hard to the top of the hill and whizzed down. The wind blew in his face and sang in his ears. For the first time he tasted the thrill of speed—glorious speed. So glorious that he was halfway down before he remembered that the road veered sharply to the right at the bottom of the hill, and he would never make the turn at the rate he was going.

Too late Tom applied the brakes. They did not grip, and the wheels tore on at a terrifying pace, spurting sand and gravel behind. He wrenched the handlebars around, shaving so close past a telegraph pole that it scraped the skin off his knuckles. His heart pounded, and he sweat with fear, but he was around the corner, and by some miracle the bicycle was still upright. The immediate steep uphill grade slowed the wheels down, permitting him to dismount.

He stood awhile, shaking like a leaf in a gale; his heart thumped so hard he thought it would burst out of his chest. By the time he stopped panting, Tom had lost all zest for bike riding. His trembling legs scarcely supported him as he wheeled the bicycle back down the hill, past the stout wooden telegraph pole. Shuddering, he realized that if he had collided with the pole at the pace he was going, not only the cycle but his head would have been smashed to smithereens.

During the long summer holidays George and Tom worked on neighboring farms, digging potatoes, harvesting, or any other odd jobs that fourteen- and fifteen-year-olds could do. They earned enough money to buy themselves candy, cigarettes, soft drinks, and all the other stuff that kids of that age consume. It never occurred to them that their money could have been put to a better use.

All these years their dad had sent money to the orphanage for their board. The government helped some when they had to be evacuated, but now they were old enough to work, and it was obvious to everyone concerned that they were not the scholastic type, so Mr. Turner sent for his sons to return to Liphook.

But before they went, Tom had another brush with death.

One evening he and George and "Hasher" McGee were plodding homeward after a day's work on a neighboring farm. Their route led over a wooden bridge spanning a narrow gully filled with water and coal-dust waste from an adjacent mine. Too thick to swim in, to thin to walk on, the stream of sludge was as dangerous as quicksand. They stopped awhile and amused themselves by throwing bits of stick and stones into the smelly black mass and watching them disappear. Tufts of grass grew up here and there through the sludge, and Hasher remarked that once he'd seen one of the local boys jump off the bridge and onto a grass tuft.

"What's so clever about that?" Tom wanted to know. "Anyone could do that."

"Oh, really, Mister Smarty-pants. Let's see you do it then."

"All right."

Without pausing to take off his heavy gum boots, Tom jumped for the nearest grass tuft—and missed.

Immediately as he landed in the sludge, his feet began to sink. There was nothing solid underneath. Nothing he could reach and hold on to. The thick ooze closed over his boots, sucking at them. He felt himself irresistibly drawn downward.

"Help!" he screamed. "I'm sinking!"

He tried to lift his feet, to pull them out of the imprisoning boots; but they were trapped. "Help!" he screamed again. "George, Hasher, help!" Frantically he grabbed at the nearest grass tuft, but it was just out of reach. "Help! Help!"

"Shut up, Tom, and keep still." Hasher took command. "You'll only sink faster if you struggle. Here, George, lie down flat on the bridge facing Tom and see if you can reach him."

George did as he was told, but Tom was still beyond his outstretched hands. Tom's panic mounted again. "Hurry! Hurry! Get a rope. Call somebody." His legs in the heavy boots sank ever deeper.

There was no house in sight. Not another human being for miles around. It would take hours to get help and by then ——"Hurry! Hurry!"

Hasher ignored Tom's cries. "George, you'll have to lean farther over the edge. I'll sit on your legs so you won't overbalance—reach out as far as you can. Tom, turn around a bit and try to grab George's hands."

The sludge held Tom's legs like a vice, but he managed to twist his body half around, and on the second attempt their hands met and held.

"Great!" Hasher threw himself on top of George and leaned far out to grasp Tom's wrists. "Hold on tight. Now, George, pull."

Hasher's grip was like iron, and the strain on Tom's outstretched arms excruciating. Sweat broke out on his forehead. Each moment was an hour of agony as their combined strength slowly drew him up until his legs were free of the boots. Inch by inch they dragged him through the filth until he was close enough to the bridge to be hauled up.

It seemed a long time that the three of them lay panting on the bridge deck, too exhausted to move. Suddenly Tom heard a horrible, sickening gurgle. He raised his head and looked over the edge. The gumboots had disappeared.

No one spoke. All three stared at the smooth surface of the gooey black sludge. Tom shivered. He wondered what else besides his boots lay hidden in its murky depths.

Tom was silent as a sphinx when the three of them set out for home. While George and Hasher talked and joked and tried to act normally, Tom shuffled along in his stockings, worrying about the lost gum boots and the state of his clothes. What could he say to Mrs. Brown? The thought of her wrath upset him more than his narrow escape. He concocted all kinds of explanations, only to discard them all when they reached the gate, because he saw that she was down at the cow barn and he could sneak in undetected.

"Tell her I'm sick and that I don't want any supper," he mumbled to George. He could hear Mr. Brown and Paddy talking in the kitchen, and his heart sank still further. There was no way he could wash or change his clothes without one of them knowing his guilty secret. In despair Tom crept into his room and climbed into bed, clothes and all, and burrowed down under the blankets.

Of course it was no use. It was so unlike Tom to miss a meal, sick or well, that Mrs. Brown became suspicious of George's story. She went into the bedroom, and when she saw the state of the bed she badgered from him the truth about the dirt and the gum boots. Then she called Paddy in, and Tom got a belting to remember.

PART THREE

Wartime Sailor

The brothers found some changes at home in Liphook. Dad appeared much the same, but Joan had grown into a tall fourteen-year-old. Aunt Julie had married a Scotsman named Jimmy McLeod, who spent a great deal of time at sea. For this reason, and because bombs fell on London nearly every night, they moved down to Liphook, where Joan attended school and Aunt Julie kept house for Dad.

His new uncle's job excited Tom's admiration. Jimmy was a bullion escort, traveling almost constantly on ships plying between England and South Africa. Tom did not know exactly what a "bullion escort" did, but he imagined that huge chests of gold and silver coins—perhaps even the crown jewels and other priceless English treasures—were being sent for safety to a distant colony until the terrible war in Europe should be over. He pictured Uncle Jimmy protecting the treasure from pirates and perils in all sorts of heroic situations.

During the boys' first few days at home the family had a lot to talk about, so much news to catch up on, so many adventures to relate. But when things settled down a bit Dad Turner made it clear that his duty was done—the boys were old enough now to support themselves, so what about it?

It was not hard for a boy to find a job when every able-bodied man was engaged in the desperate war for survival. No one worried about Tom's past scholastic record or his future ambitions. As long as he could obey instructions, and be quick about it, he was considered satisfactory. He soon found a job as office boy at BRECO (British Ropeways Engineering

Company), a London firm that moved out during the Battle of Britain and established itself in a grand old country estate, in Hampshire.

George found work as an office boy, too, but he did not stay long. As soon as he turned sixteen he joined the navy in the Fleet Air Arm branch.

That made Tom green with envy. There was George in uniform and getting ready to win the war while he licked stamps and emptied wastepaper baskets. It was insufferable. He brooded over the injustice of it all. Why couldn't he and George have been born twins? Every day the situation became more unbearable, until finally Tom had one of his bright ideas.

He knew where Dad kept his receipts and insurance policies and other important papers, and as soon as he had the chance, he leafed through them until he found the birth certificate of Thomas Trussler Turner.

With a trembling hand he altered the date from March 11, 1927, to March 11, 1926. Next day he skipped work and jubilantly set off for the Portsmouth recruiting office to enlist in the navy.

Tom's heart thumped like mad while he waited in line with the sixteen-year-olds, and when his turn came he tried to act as nonchalant as they. But the recruiting officer, an old sea dog with a stunning array of medals on his chest and a jagged scar across his forehead, took one look at the doctored birth certificate and Tom's beardless face and barked, "Go home, lad. Come again when you're sixteen."

Tom tried to protest, but the officer waved him off and turned to the next applicant. Tom could do nothing but return, glowering and muttering, to his office-boy job in Liphook and his youthful search for excitement.

Dad Turner might have washed his hands as far as supporting his boys went, but he still felt responsible for them. Tom caused him a lot of concern. The boy did not know the meaning of danger. As fast as he survived one reckless exploit, he was into another.

"Keep him busy," Aunt Julie suggested. "Don't leave him any time to get out with other boys and look for mischief."

No sooner said than done. Mrs. White, the old family friend out at the Deer's Hut Inn, had been widowed early in the war, and she needed help on the weekends. Mr. Turner himself often helped her out, and it was easy enough to persuade Tom that he could use extra money.

Tom wiped tables, washed glasses, served beer—helped with anything that needed doing. Whenever kind Mrs. White was not looking, he saw no harm in helping himself to a pack of cigarettes or a little extra money from the till.

The Deer's Hut was popular with the army men. As well as the British camp out at Longmoore, there were a lot of Canadian troops nearby. They were a great bunch, and Tom became friendly with all of them. They called him "the kid," and gave him a lot of cheek. He cheeked them right back.

Tom's special friend was Joe, a short, stocky black boy. Tom and he used to fool around a lot, elbow each other around, tease, and crack jokes.

One evening Tom was collecting glasses in the barroom where Joe and some of his buddies were drinking, and as usual they exchanged some lip. Tom carried his tray of glasses outside, and when he returned Joe was in the middle of telling a long tale of some narrow escape he'd had, when Tom broke in:

"Yah, Joe, you'd be safe. No one could see you on a dark night."

Before Tom closed his mouth, Joe whipped out a knife and sprang for his throat. Luckily for Tom, Joe's buddies reacted just as quick. They grabbed the black and wrestled him outside before any damage was done.

Tom gaped after them. The shock of Joe's fury and sudden attack stunned him. Whatever had happened that Joe should attack one of his best friends like that?

He realized later that Joe had been drunk, and the next time they met, the soldier was as friendly and teasing as ever. But for many nights afterward Tom had only to close his eyes to see again the hate blazing in Joe's eyes and the flash of steel, bright in the lamplight.

The incident shook Mrs. White, too, and she took Tom aside and warned him to be more careful.

"You could have been murdered, Tom," she said. "It's a miracle he didn't kill you."

No amount of wishing on Tom's part made the time go any faster, and it seemed like eternity, waiting for the months to drag by until his sixteenth birthday. But at last it came round, and he presented himself once more at the naval recruiting office. This time he was accepted without question, given a number, an outfit, and was assigned to a shore establishment—he was in the navy.

The new recruits did not go straight to sea. They had hundreds of things to learn before they were even allowed aboard the one-and-a-half-ton training cutters moored in a huge swimming pool.

Even then, when the landlubbers among the recruits went aboard to learn how to row a boat, they were set to practice with oars that had holes in them so that the water swished through. They expended a great deal of sweat and energy and went nowhere.

Ten rookies comprised a crew. When their instructors thought they could row well enough to handle a small boat, they took the boys out to sea. They learned how to hoist a sail and the difference between mainsails and foresails and jibs. This was more exciting than being moored in a swimming pool, and Tom enjoyed every moment of it.

"This navy is real man's stuff," he wrote in one of his rare letters home. His father sensed his enthusiasm and shook his head in bewildered fashion.

"That boy was such a washout at school, I thought he'd hate the discipline of naval life. It just goes to show . . ."

While Dad Turner was pondering over the unpredictability of his younger son, Tom was finding out that seamanship, at least in wartime, included learning about mines, depth charges, torpedoes, and guns. In one room a six-inch shell, weighing over a hundred pounds and nicknamed "Percy" occupied pride of place. Not only did the instructors use Percy for classroom demonstrations, but they also found him a valuable aid in maintaining discipline.

Sometimes the classroom atmosphere had a demoralizing effect on the crew, and they tended to cut up like a bunch of naughty schoolboys. Then the class instructor singled out the ringleader and roared, "O.S.* Jones, hold Percy!" and the chagrined youth had to come to the front, pick up the heavy shell and hold it for the remainder of the class period. If he sagged ever so slightly the officer noticed it and roared, "Hup! Stand up!"

Practice followed theory, and the officers took their crews out to a lonely spot on the coast of Wales, where they could shoot out to sea with reasonable assurance of not hitting anything.

Tom's crew were training on a six-inch gun that took a shell like Percy. This particular gun took a separate shell and charge, and it had to be fired by hand. Their petty officer showed them how to take hold of the lanyard, pull it taut, and then strike it a sharp blow with the fist to make it fire. Again and again he warned them to stand well back because the gun's recoil was about forty inches, and if any fellow got in the way of that, all his troubles would be over.

Day after day the petty officer put his crew through their paces. The boys went through the drill over and over again—changing places, each member of the gun crew learning to do each function. Then came time for the actual firing, and Tom gulped with excitement. They used *real* shells that made a terrific noise—the flash and the bang made the crew feel terribly important. Tom saw by the looks on their faces that they felt as confident as he—they could win the war all by themselves if the need arose.

Once more they all took their places, and the petty officer

---

*Ordinary Seaman.

looked them over and unexpectedly asked, "Who is the youngest in this crew?"

A hasty whispering revealed that Tom was the youngest by a few months, and he raised his hand.

"Right. Turner, you do the firing."

Tom stepped forward, unsure whether he was being honored or belittled. Whichever it was, he determined to show the officer that he knew his drill. Smartly he took up the lanyard and waited while the crew pushed in the shell and closed the breech. Then he pulled the lanyard taut, doubled his fist, and struck a mightly blow.

But the blow did not turn out nearly as hard as he intended, and the vent-sealing tube refused to fire.

Tom tried again and still nothing happened.

None of the fellows snickered—they would not dare in front of the petty officer—but Tom sensed that they were bursting inside over his discomfiture.

Red to the ears, he struck again. And again. Still nothing happened. Tom's exertions were getting him nowhere, except closer and closer to the gun breech.

"Tug it!" The petty officer rapped out.

Tom gave a mighty heave on the lanyard, and the same instant that the gun fired the petty officer leaped forward and hurled the boy aside. The gun breech whistled past with not an inch to spare.

It all happened too quickly for Tom to feel anything but surprise; however, the petty officer turned pale and swore under his breath a few times before he regained his composure and turned to the gaping gun crew. "See what could have happened? Let this be a lesson to all of you. REMEMBER to stand back from the breech."

Another part of the training was learning to fire a gun in the dark. Tom and his mates had no idea what was ahead the day the instructor herded them into a small, windowless room where several other officers waited behind a gun. The instructor left the door open while he assigned their places and told them what to do. Tom glimpsed a large sheet of corrugated iron suspended above their heads. He wondered why it was there, but this was no time for indulging curiosity; the instructor was looking in his direction.

"Turner, you be captain."

This gun was of a slightly different type. Tom had to open the breech, then while one of the other lads loaded, Tom took a vent-sealing tube and put it in place to fire the charge. When the other lad shouted, "Loaded!" Tom slammed the breech shut. The other boy had to make sure his fingers were out of the way, because when the breech shut, the great wheels inside it turned and locked.

It was a dangerous procedure at any time. The instructor put them through the drill three or four times—whamming the dummy shells into the breech; banging the door; turning the wheel; firing—until they could do it accurately and automatically.

"Right," he said, and slammed the door. Before their eyes grew accustomed to the eerie darkness, he shouted "Fire!" and they bent to the task.

With only their sense of touch to rely on, the crew loaded the gun and fired. Tom nearly hit the roof as the roar of explosion in that confined space almost burst his eardrums. For a split second he was mystified. How could dummy shells make such a row? Suddenly a flare lit up the instructor's face, and Tom realized that he was tossing firecrackers in among them as he yelled: "Keep firing!"

They kept firing. Working like machines, they opened, loaded, closed, fired. Their sweaty faces shone with grim resolve in the intermittent flashes of vivid light. Tom's ears reverberated to the fearful din of the explosions, and he wondered how the others were making out. A torrent of water cascaded down, soaking him to the skin, and he knew what the corrugated iron was for.

"Keep firing!"

Tom kept doggedly on with his part of the routine, only to jump again at a sudden burst of shrapnel on his right and the growling roll of simulated gunfire behind him. The noise and confusion all about in the darkness was calculated to make the stoutest heart quail, but still the intructor yelled above the din, "Keep firing!"

At last it was all over, and the instructor opened the door, letting light into the room of simulated hell. Tom blinked and looked around to see what had made those terrible noises. One petty officer held a long narrow metal box half-filled with gravel. As he tilted it back and forth the gravel shot from end to end making a sound like bursts of shrapnel fire. Another petty officer manipulated a large sheet of metal strung with piano wires. He shook and rattled this weird contraption until it sounded like the wind howling and moaning against a background of thunder.

Tom realized that this was all done to train the gun crew to act under actual combat conditions when they would have to stick to their guns no matter what distractions surrounded them.

The commando course was calculated to make men out of boys. From the beginning of their training, two or three mornings a week the rookies ran for miles through the woods to toughen themselves up. The first time they went out breakfastless; Tom's stomach pinched and grumbled, and he grew so weak with hunger that he thought he would never make it. They were not allowed to carry so much as a toffee or a canteen of water with them. And they couldn't slacken their pace, even if they happened to pass an edible berry bush.

Gradually he got used to that exercise, and then they were ordered to run in battle dress, complete with packs and rifles. That was bad enough, but next came the order to cross a single cable strung over a canyon.

Once safely over the canyon, Tom had no time to congratulate himself; the officers urged them on, and Tom dashed full speed toward a twelve-foot-high wall. The first two men to reach it grasped their rifles firmly and made a step so that the third fellow could jump onto it, and with a helping heave from them, added to his own momentum, he was almost thrown over the wall.

One of the fellows in Tom's crew broke his leg the first time he went over. That caused some consternation, and the rest of them learned to hurdle it safely by clutching at the top of the wall as they went over and sliding down the other side.

There was no respite. Without a moment's break to catch their breath, as soon as they cleared the wall, the rookies had to run full pelt up a ramp that overlooked a great bath of water, then jump clear. Woe betide the one who fell in or let his rifle touch the ground.

What next? Tom wondered as he cleared the water jump and panted toward a low hummock riddled with holes like large rabbit burrows. He made for the nearest hole. The circumference was scarcely large enough to admit a man and his pack, but obviously the commandos-to-be were expected to go through.

Tom adjusted his pack and crawled in. His body blocked out the light, and the earthy smell reminded him of his childhood tunnel digging. He wormed forward on his stomach. His rifle kept poking into the tunnel roof, and when he tried to ease it around and get it under his arm, it dug into the wall.

Cursing, he backed until he freed the rifle. He closed his eyes against the falling dirt and inched himself forward again. Slowly, slowly. The tunnel closed about him, constricting, suffocating. Tom wondered how Dougal was getting on. Dougal suffered from claustrophobia. Tom didn't, but all the same he felt like screaming, "Let me out of here!"

His groping fingers found a root and closed around it. He levered himself forward. His pack jammed in a narrow place. He held his breath and made his body as flat as possible. He jerked free. Another meter, two . . . He opened his eyes and saw the welcome glimmer of daylight ahead.

Triumphantly Tom dragged himself out into the clear, fresh air, stamped a few times to shake off the loose earth, and ran toward the next hurdle.

Already one of his mates was there, balancing arms outstretched like a tightrope walker as he teetered his way across a slender pole spanning a deep canyon.

The pole seemed to be the last straw for a lot of the fellows. The heavy packs made balancing difficult, and Tom watched in dismay as first Dougal and then McPherson lost their balance and tumbled into the canyon. The next one across dropped his rifle, and the next one lost his pack. Tom drew a deep breath, settled his pack squarely in the center of his back, and ran for the pole.

His aggressive tactic paid off, and he crossed safely, only to find himself running slap-bang into a sheer cliff. Ropes dangled from the top of the cliff. Tom panted to the nearest one and began to climb. The first few yards were easy enough, then his boot slipped on the rock face, and he swung like a pendulum. He clung desperately to the rope and hauled himself a few inches higher, kicking at the cliff face until he found another foothold—and another.

His pack and rifle made him feel top-heavy; his unyielding boots could not have been more unsuitable climbing gear; his hands cramped and burned; but he gritted his teeth and clambered upward until he was able to throw himself over the top and see what lay ahead.

He looked, and for one chilling moment his blood seemed to curdle in his veins. Only yards away a row of enemy soldiers in full battle dress faced him. Tom gasped, then grinned. Dummies, of course. Now what were the instructions concerning them?

Don't charge alone. Wait until your comrades have climbed the cliff. Aim for a vital spot.

Tom looked around. Heads were popping up all along the cliff.

"Come on, fellows!" he yelled, and dashed forward to thrust his bayonet into the sawdust enemy's vitals. But even that was not the end of the course. There were more water jumps and sand jumps and hoops and holes and hollows to jump in or over or crawl through. Most of the recruits passed their commando course creditably. Young Tom Turner did so well that when the next batch came in for training, his officers had him repeat the course to show the rookies how it was done.

As the months flew by, Tom found that seamanship was only a small part of a naval recruit's training. A seemingly endless list of different courses stretched ahead of him, but he had a mind to learn and tackled them all with gusto. By the time Tom was seventeen and a half he was an ordinary seaman, the lowest rung on the ladder of rank. He nearly burst with pride when he wrote his father of his accomplishment: "It won't be long now, Dad. I'll be a rear admiral before you know it."

Now Tom and his mates felt that they were real men. They acted big. They smoked and drank and swore. They told risqué yarns and spit and ogled the girls. One night when they had leave from their billet in one of the famous Billy Butlin Holiday Camps in Skegness, Lincolnshire, a crowd of them descended on the local hotel.

Near the hotel door a weather-beaten old sailor with a wooden leg held out his grimy cap: "Help an old tar, Jack.* Help an old tar."

He clinked his few coins pathetically, and the boisterous newcomers dug into their pockets and half-filled his cap as they pushed through the swinging doors.

Inside, the large saloon was decorated in old-time sea fashion. Huge wall paintings of famous sea battles showed ships with broken masts and shredded rigging and the heroic sailors repulsing attacking armadas. Fiery daubs in the sky traced bursting shells or cannonballs.

Above the bar, framed sketches of pirates and buccaneers frowned from their vantage point; and ropes and rigging and nets dangled from the ceiling. Rusty iron anchors and wooden barrels leaning in the corners lent such a hearty, salty air to the place that Tom felt like leaping onto a stool and yelling, "Yo-ho-ho, and a bottle of rum."

Mac spied an empty table, and the whole group descended

---

*British slang for any sailor.

59

on it, dragging up extra chairs, shouting and shoving and guffawing, showing off their toughness.

Hefty, middle-aged barmaids hurried from table to table of the crowded bar, keeping the beer mugs full and the pockets empty. The loud laughter and talk increased in tempo as the night wore on and the air grew blue with more than tobacco smoke.

While he was leaning back in his chair laughing at one of Mac's jokes, Tom happened to look toward the door and caught sight of the old sailor unstrapping his wooden leg. He straightened his real leg, rubbed the back of his knee a couple of time, and rolled toward the bar.

Tom nearly choked—the old duper! Adding so much atmosphere to the place. "Fellows," he croaked. "Look at him! Look at the cunning old beggar. He's got two good legs . . ."

Tom's companions craned around to look and roar their appreciation.

"It's hi—hi—hilarious," Mac hiccuped. "Here, fella, have a drink. It's on me."

They crowded around the old tar and dragged him to their table, slapping him on the back and shouting him drinks to loosen his tongue. They were amply repaid. The old salt entertained them with wild and improbable tales of his seafaring days until the bar closed and they staggered campward to sleep off their binge and awaken soreheaded in the morning.

The recruits went wild with excitement when the long-awaited orders to embark arrived. They laughed and cheered and slapped one another's back, made the victory sign with their fingers, and exclaimed again and again that now the war would soon be over.

They were not quite so enthusiastic by the time they boarded the train for the trip across England. It was midwinter, the war was in its fifth year with almost everything rationed—particularly fuel. During their training days the lads had been too busy to notice the cold, but now, sitting all night in a dimly lit, unheated troop train, they nearly froze.

They piled on all their heavy winter clothes so that they looked as bulky as a bunch of grizzly bears—and grizzle they did. But no amount of griping or swearing could alter the situation. As the night wore on, the cold grew even more intense. Some of the fellows used their greatcoats as blankets and huddled together on the floor trying to sleep. Others climbed onto the overhead luggage racks and stretched out, but a couple of the racks broke and spilled them and their packs down onto their prone mates, increasing the confusion.

Because of the enforcement of a strict blackout, petty officers patrolled the carriages to ensure that no one smoked or struck a match unless the shutters were tightly drawn.

Despite his boyhood spent in Scotland's cold climate, Tom shivered along with the rest. While the unheated train chugged carefully across the winter-white countryside, he spent most of the long bitter night in the corridor clapping his hands and stomping his feet to keep his blood circulating.

Miserable as they felt, the lads managed a cheer when they arrived at Liverpool docks and the petty officers herded them aboard a great Dutch hulk named *Indrapora*. They dumped their packs in the barrackslike cabins and swarmed over the ship—their first *real* ship—as excited as schoolboys. Their excitement mounted when they discovered that the *Indrapora* carried a number of German prisoners of war, who were being shipped off to South Africa or Australia, anywhere to get them as far away as possible from the theater of war.

Tom and his mates felt that they grew inches during those first few hours aboard. With their training days over, now they'd show the enemy how the British lion could roar. They stood around the deck in little groups learnedly discussing sea-battle tactics or speculating on their probable destination, until, under cover of darkness, the *Indrapora* weighed anchor and steamed off—straight into the teeth of a gale.

The newcomers aboard soon shrank to their former size when their petty officers sent most of them down to the galley to help the cooks. It was hot in there, and as steamy as a tropical jungle. Full of smells and noise, it was not at all the sort of place for a batch of recruits experiencing their first storm at sea.

The head chef, a huge Dutchman whose tall white hat brushed the maze of pipes crisscrossing the deckhead, greeted them cheerily and set them to work. They peeled onions until their eyes had no tears left. "Dutch" noted their sniveling discomfiture and threw his head back and laughed so hard that he had to clasp his hands over his enormous wobbling stomach.

Some of the fellows were affected by more than onion odor. At every roll of the ship their faces turned a shade paler, and they gulped and swallowed in desperate efforts to stave off seasickness. Big Dutch noticed that, too, and shouted at them:

"Looka 'ere, you fellas."

When all eyes in the galley turned on him he dipped his massive paw into a pot of stew and fished out a large, greasy lump of fat and guzzled it down, smacking his lips and making a great show of enjoyment. His little sideshow had the desired effect, and he burst into hoots of laughter as the squeamish ones dashed from the galley with their hands tightly clamped over mouths and heaving stomachs.

Rough seas did not bother Tom. He seemed to be a born sailor and stood with legs apart and body braced against the ship's roll, while he chopped vegetables, stirred stew, sliced bread, and did whatever other task Dutch set for him. And all the while he worked his thoughts kept straying back to a picture on the wall of the common room at Dean Orphange.

It was a picture of a ship sailing toward a tropical island so bright with sun and sand that it dazzled the eyes. Tom loved to stand and look at it on dull days when snow coated the Scottish lawns and frost misted the windows. He used to wonder whether someday he might travel to far away places where the sky was blue and cloudless, like it was in the painting, and not eternally gray like it was in Scotland.

And now at last he was bound for an unknown destination

that in all probability was in the tropics, and might even be an island.

From Liverpool the *Indrapora* steamed down the Mersey to join a large convoy of merchant ships and destroyers in the Irish Sea before venturing south into the Atlantic. Enemy submarines dogged the shipping lanes, and every ship in the convoy was eyes and ears for every other ship. The ships were camouflaged to make them less visible in daylight, and at night they observed a strict blackout.

But one night the lookout on an accompanying destroyer noticed flashes of light streaming from the direction of the *Indrapora*. He watched for a while until he was convinced that the light was not an accidental violation of the blackout but a series of deliberate signals. He informed his superiors, who alerted the captain of the *Indrapora* by radio, and he sent an officer to search below decks.

The officer went below to the hold, and it did not take him long to discover that some of the prisoners of war had wrenched open one of the heavy porthole covers and were opening and closing it at long and short intervals, sending coded light signals far out across the dark seas in the hope of attracting one of their own ships or planes.

Tom was dumbfounded when that bit of news leaked out around the ship. Surely the Germans weren't *that* patriotic! Didn't they realize that if the *Indrapora* was sunk, they would go down too?

There were a number of SS troopers among the prisoners of war on board, and they were kept under tight guard, the captain taking no chances with them. But some of the other prisoners were lads about Tom's age or a little older, and he and his mates often talked to them. A great many of them spoke English, some had even been educated at Oxford, and Tom marveled at the way they had been brainwashed in their own country. They simply would not believe it when Tom told them that the war was almost over and that they were on the losing side. They would not listen to a word against Hitler.

"Just propaganda," they laughed at him. "Your Churchill is not telling the truth. Germany will be victorious. *Deutschland über alles!*"

It was impossible to convince them, even though there were shortwave radios on board, and after each important broadcast, Tom or some of his mates relayed the world news to them as it came from the front by way of the BBC. The Germans were so impregnated with Nazism they could not believe that Hitler had failed.

Day after day the *Indrapora* steamed on toward an undisclosed destination. The weather grew milder, the sky more blue and cloudless, and Tom's mood more carefree. This is the life, he mused, leaning over the ship's rail, watching the water frothing past the bow; the warm breeze fluttering his short sleeves and ruffling his hair. Pity the rest of them freezing back there in England.

Apart from the daily lifeboat drills, kitchen fatigue, and other duties the officers devised to keep the men occupied, Tom thought the voyage through the Bay of Biscay was one big pleasure cruise. He was sorry when he and most of the other sailors disembarked at Gibraltor and joined the naval base at Catalan Bay.

Part of the navy's job there was to patrol the Strait of Gibraltar, discouraging saboteurs, who had the nasty habit of sneaking in from the Spanish coast and causing a great deal of damage. One of their favorite tricks was to dive down at night and attach limpet mines to unsuspecting Allied ships. Spain was not actively involved in the war, but she was friendly toward Germany and turned a blind eye on the saboteur's activities.

Britain had suffered so much during the long years of war that the naval contingent at Gibraltar consisted largely of a motley collection of craft that were never intended for the use to which they were now being put. For part of his time there Tom was one of the crew manning a large yacht that, he was told, once belonged to the film star Errol Flynn. The captain was easygoing, and as long as his crew worked well he made few rules, with the result that when they were not on duty they had the time of their young lives.

Tom swam in the warm Mediterranean waters and basked on deck in the dazzling sunshine. When he had shore leave he and his mates got special Spanish permits and went off to see the bullfights in La Linea and Algeciras. They had plenty of fun and food, and at times they forgot the pains of war, the food rationing, and the hard life of their friends and relatives in poor old England.

But at other times they saw terrible sights. Tom soon realized that, though war seems so gallant and glorious to read about, living through it is a different matter. He was not involved in actual conflict, but he saw enough to know that behind the glamour and the glory there lurked brutal death and destruction.

Often the captain received orders to steam out into the Atlantic and search for survivors after a ship had been torpedoed by the enemy. Given the exact longitude and latitude positions from the last radio contact with the doomed ship, their craft plowed full steam ahead until they reached the place. Then, with spotters in the crow's nest using binoculars and the rest of the crew lining the rails, they circled around and looked for survivors in lifeboats or those clinging to wreckage. The many lives saved were only a small percentage compared with those who were killed or drowned, and even some of the rescued men died later from their injuries.

Tankers were the worst. Tom shuddered when he knew that a tanker had gone down. He knew what they would find at the terrible scene—a flaming film of spilled oil spreading out over the water. There was no escaping it. Most of the men picked up were frightfully burned: every particle of hair gone, their skin sloughing off from blisters and exposure to salt water. They screamed in agony as they were hauled aboard, and Tom wondered whether, after all, drowning might have been less painful than rescue.

One time when Tom's little convoy was reconnoitering off the coast of Greece, one of their own ships hit a mine and blew up right in front of their horrified eyes. Only four survivors were picked up, and they were crazy with shock and had to be restrained. The orderlies bundled them into sick bay, and the ship went on cruising around, picking up the parts of bodies that floated among the wreckage. They found the captain's arm still wearing the sleeve with all the gold braid attached. They hauled up quite a lot before the sharks moved in, and the officers took all the collected limbs and pieces of bodies ashore and gave them proper burial.

Weeks lengthened into months, and for much of the time nothing noteworthy happened. The ships anchored in the harbor awaiting orders, and the crews grew bored and restless. Rumor had it that the war was nearly over, but officialdom remained tight-lipped on the subject.

For some time Tom's ship had been moored in Trieste harbor, and with little to do on board the crew had more shore leave than was good for them.

There were servicemen's clubs in Trieste, as well as plenty of saloons. Most of the crews spent their shore leave drinking or dancing with the "good-time girls." Sometimes gangs of sailors and soldiers got together and wandered up and down the streets looking for excitement. With hundreds of Allied naval and military personnel based in the vicinity, and a mixed local population of Italians and Yugoslavians who, no matter what neutrality their politicians vowed, were definitely pro-German, it was not hard to stir up trouble.

The Italians, especially some of the fanatically political groups, got terribly worked up when they saw Italian girls walking out with the Allies. They shook their fists and threatened and yelled, and a real war of words ensued. Usually they did not dare to start a fight because most of the Allied servicemen carried guns, but if they managed to grab the girls involved, they shaved their heads, stripped off their clothes, and sent them home in disgrace.

For no reason that Tom or anyone else could put into words, a lot of jealousy existed between the British and

American forces based near Trieste, and if either group were bored, they found it easy enough to start some excitement. Gangs of British eighteen- and nineteen-year-olds deliberately sat at quayside cafés in the shadow of nearby American ships, sipped drinks, and thumbed their noses at the U.S. Marines.

The marines, responding with a shower of empty bottles, shouted, "Take that you so-and-so Limeys."

And the Limeys threw the bottles back and yelled taunts: "Yah, you yellow Yanks, come down and fight like men!"

Never shy of such an invitation, the marines swarmed down, and the café became a battlefield. Chairs and tables were overturned, crockery and glassware smashed, food and drink spattered everywhere, as a score or so Allies punched and kicked and blasphemed each other. The poor café proprietor dodged in and out among them, wringing his hands and shrieking, "Non, non, signors."

This sort of incident was not listed in official records or reported in the newspapers "at home," but a lot of fellows classed as battle casualties were injured, even killed, in street fights and hooliganisms that had nothing to do with the war.

One evening at twilight when Tom sauntered down the street toward the Army, Navy, and Air Force Club, hoping to find a couple of mates to help him pass the time, he rounded a corner and almost knocked into an American soldier carrying a gun.

"Careful," he grunted and tried to sidestep, but the soldier grabbed his shoulder and poked the gun into his stomach.

It was done in such true gangster-film fashion that Tom thought the man was joking, but one look at the wild gleam in his eyes revealed that he was either drunk or mad. Instinctively Tom wanted to break free and run, but he knew the soldier would shoot if he did. He kept quiet and tried to remain calm. If the man was mad, he would have to try and humor him.

Without relaxing his iron grip on Tom's shoulder, the soldier prodded the gun harder and growled: "Buddy, can you speak American?"

Tom gulped. "No, I speak English."

The soldier thrust his face close and glared. The gun pressed harder. Tom closed his eyes and thought his last hour had come. For seconds that seemed like hours they stood like that, then the wild-eyed soldier grunted and moved on.

Tom moved too. He broke all records getting to the club-rooms.

That was not Tom's only narrow escape at Trieste. One night he was lounging in his cabin, smoking and reading, when Mac came in.

"Wanta see something?" Mac grinned and kept one hand behind his back.

"Of course." Tom jerked to a sitting position. "What've you got?"

Trying his best to look mysterious Mac slowly brought his hand to the front and held up a gun. "Isn't it a beauty?"

Tom whistled between his teeth. "Sure is. Where'd you get it?"

"Bought it from an old Itie." Mac polished the barrel with his sleeve and held the gun up so that the light glinted off the metal. "Works like a little beauty, too." He took the magazine out and pointed the unloaded gun straight at Tom, "Stick 'em up, Jack!"

Entering into the spirit of the game, Tom threw his hands in the air and cried, "Non, non, signor; don'ta shoota me! I maka you da spaghetti——"

He was good at mimicking the Italians, and Mac went into peals of laughter at his antics and pulled the trigger.

There was a report that sounded like cannon fire in such close quarters, and Tom thought that he was shot.

He could not believe his eyes when he looked down and saw no gaping hole in his tunic and no blood gushing out. He stared stupidly at his middle and wondered where the bullet went in, wondered why he did not fall over dead.

"Are you all right?" Mac's voice sounded hoarse, and his frightened eyes burned in his pale face.

"I—I—think so."

Tom passed a hand gingerly over his chest, shoulders, stomach. He staggered to his feet, clutching at the bunk above for support. He still could not believe that he was unhurt. The gun had pointed directly at his heart.

"You forgot the one in the breech," he accused, and Mac nodded dumbly.

Too shocked to talk, they stood and stared at each other. Except for the bullet lodged in the woodwork behind him, everything in the cabin looked the same as it had ten minutes earlier, but the thoughts kept whirling around Tom's head, "I could have been dead now. What if we hadn't fooled? What if Mac hadn't laughed so hard and spoiled his aim?"

In the middle of his whirling thoughts he seemed to hear voices from the past—women's voices: Mrs. Landers saying, "It's a miracle he wasn't killed." The market women at Dean village, "It's a miracle . . . " Mrs. White in the old Deer's Hut, "It's a miracle he didn't kill you, Tom."

A miracle. A miracle.

Tom swallowed hard at something that seemed to stick in his throat, and suddenly he was blurting out to Mac all the narrow escapes he'd had in his life, beginning with being hit by a truck when he was just a few years old. He showed Mac the scars.

"Wow!" he blinked. "There must be a reason for it, Tom. You've got more lives than a cat!"

Tom and his mates were back in Gibraltar when the war with Germany ended, and the whole base went wild with excitement. The petty officers kept reminding them that there was still Japan to clean up, but the score with Hitler was settled, and that was something the lads were determined to celebrate. For the most part the officers ignored their wild goings-on because they had fine shenanigans of their own. For days there was scarcely a sober man on base. Rumors flew from bunk to bunk, and speculations salted every conversation as to how soon the men could expect to be back in Blighty (Britain).

There were plenty of sore heads when VE Day ended. For weeks afterward the frenzied excitement broke out afresh whenever a German U-boat slunk into the harbor with a British flag draped over its German flag.

"Yah!" Tom exulted, wishing with all his heart that he could meet up with those young Nazi prisoners of war from the *Indrapora* who had been so sure that their "Faderland" was invincible. How he would crow over them!

Not long after VE Day Tom and some of his mates were transferred to a BYMS (Brooklyn Yard Mine Sweeper), a slow-moving wooden tub that took a crew of twenty-five to thirty men. Once again they had a captain who was a "good sort." He left the crew pretty much to their own devices during the slow voyage around the Mediterranean. After the necessary duties were done, the crew passed the days fishing, wisecracking, drinking, and swimming.

It was Tom's friend, MacDonald, who had the brain wave about swimming.

A row of lads leaned over the rail one sizzling day watching the tantalizingly cool water curling and frothing under the bows, and someone said:

"Man, I'd like a swim."

"Well, why not?" asked MacDonald. "This tub is slow enough that anyone could swim alongside and keep up with it."

"You're mad!" some of the fellows howled at him. "What about the sharks?"

"Sharks?" Oh, they're easily fixed. You throw a hand grenade into the sea, and that scares them off."

Mac had to do a lot of talking before he convinced his listeners that someone of unimpeachable authority had given him the information; and by that time someone else in the group remembered having heard the same thing, and finally the crew decided to chance it.

In a body they approached the skipper and asked him to stop the engines for a while. Good sport that he was, he complied; and Mac hurried below to fetch a couple of hand grenades.

The fellows lined the rail and watched as Mac tossed the grenades over and saw them explode in an eruption of bubbles far below. Whooping with delight, they stripped off their sweaty uniforms and dived in.

Tom hesitated for a moment, hoping Mac was right about the efficacy of underwater explosions, then he dived in with the rest. The water felt as cool as it looked, and after a while he stopped having a near heart attack every time a bit of flotsam bumped his bare skin and began really enjoying himself.

"This is the life," he yelled, treading water and blowing mouthfuls of salt spray at his mates. They retaliated, and the fun and frolic that went on proved irresistible to some of the perspiring officers, who forgot their dignity and dived overboard to join the school of porpoiselike humans.

But the fun and fine weather did not last. A day out from Malta they ran into one of the fierce storms for which the Mediterranean Sea is famous.

Tom was with a group ordered up to secure one of the deck awnings that had torn loose. Within minutes the combination of rain and sea spray soaked him to the skin. He clung to the safety ropes strung along the deckhouse and wondered how the old tub stood the strain. Every timber creaked and groaned as the little vessel bucked the rearing waves, and everything that was not securely battened down crashed and clattered with the force of the gale.

The wind howled through the rigging, and the wet awning lashed his face and tore off his fingernails as he struggled to leash its writhing fury. In the middle of the turmoil Tom looked leeward in the gray blur of rain and sea and made out the shape of an Italian passenger ship plowing past. He rushed to the rail and gave it a rousing cheer, which no one but his own group heard. They left the awning to its frenzied flappings and slid across the deck to join him.

The presence of a Lloyd Triestino passenger ship, without escort, was convincing evidence that the war in Europe really was over, and the fellows cheered and waved and excitedly shook hands with one another and slapped Tom on the back and congratulated him as if he had been the one who put the ship there.

Half a day later the storm blew itself out, and the ship anchored at Messina, Sicily.

Despite all hopes and rumors, official communications revealed no plans for naval withdrawal from the Mediterranean. Instead, the Brooklyn Yard Mine Sweepers received orders to clear the sea-lanes of mines.

In some cases Intelligence had captured German plans and knew the exact location of the mines. It was a comparatively easy matter for the navy to sweep these up and defuse them. But mostly the little ships had to cruise around and around, searching the sea, never knowing at what moment they might hit a mine and blow up.

It was little wonder that tempers shortened in the tense atmosphere that prevailed aboard, and it was a relief to all when the ship returned to base at Trieste and the crew enjoyed an overdue shore leave.

Trieste was known as "the Jewel of the Adriatic," though Tom privately regarded it as a pretty tarnished sort of jewel. As usual, he and his mates went to the nearest bar and drank themselves silly. When it came time to return to ship Tom could not make it.

Along with the others he stumbled out of the hotel and staggered his way down the street until they came to a tiny park. Enticed by the sight of soft grass shining in the moonlight, Tom said thickly, "Just leave me here, fellash. I—I'll have a li'l shleep before I go back."

He slumped down in the shadow of a great tree, and no amount of tugging and pulling moved him.

"Leave him then," grunted Mac. "Serve him right if he's put in the clink."

It was long past midnight when a hearty kick in the backside interrupted Tom's snores. He forced his bleary eyes open and saw the base commander and a military policeman standing over him. Sudden fright surged through him, and he scrabbled the grass in urgent efforts to scramble to his feet and salute; but the CO turned away in disgust. "Get this so-and-so sailor back to his ship," he commanded.

The MP obeyed with gusto. None too gently he hustled Tom into a dinghy and sent him back to his ship.

Sobered a little by that narrow escape from trouble, Tom did not go ashore for a couple of nights; so he happened to be leaning over the ship's rail one evening when he heard a cabin door bang open and turned in time to see "Sparks," the wireless operator, hurrying toward the captain's cabin. It was not long before word passed around that Intelligence reported sixty mines laid in the harbor of Pula, and the captain's orders were to go with all speed and sink them.

By the time the crew ashore were rounded up, the barometer had fallen, and when at last the little ship weighed anchor a terrific storm raged. Tom knew the captain would not relish putting to sea in such a gale, but a glance at the map showed that Pula was nearly a day's steaming away, and he knew that delay could mean disaster for any unsuspecting Allied ships that might put into Pula harbor.

The ship tossed like a cork on the boisterous waves, and many even of the seasoned sailors got seasick.

On these small ships the crew took turns at any task, and during the storm it fell Tom's lot to be cook. But how could he cook food when it was all he could do to remain upright and when nothing could stand on the seesawing stove? Pots and pans clattered and crashed in the galley, cutlery rattled in the drawers, and for twenty-four hours no one had anything hot to eat or drink. By some miracle Tom managed to slice bread for corn-beef sandwiches without cutting off his fingers. These sandwiches served to sustain those who were well enough to man the essential chores.

No amount of tossing and swaying made Tom seasick, and he went from one part of the ship to another lending a hand wherever he could. At 11 AM Doble, the chief engine-room artificer, who was also helping around, called him to help distribute the midmorning rum ration. Most of the fellows were so ill they just moaned, "I don't want it. You can have mine."

What luck! Tom quaffed so many unwanted rum rations that he could hardly stand, and Doble was not much better. Chuckling foolishly, they finished their round and then decided to go up on deck for a breath of fresh air. Below decks the combined smells of engine oil and vomit were enough to turn the strongest stomach, and they were not taking any chances.

Donning sou'westers they clambered up the companionway and pushed up the hatch. It was too dangerous near the rail where the force of waves broke over the deck; so they kept close to the lifelines and hand over hand worked their way along, breathing great drafts of clean, fresh air. Suddenly Doble, who had been a singer at the Royal Opera House in Covent Garden took it into his head to sing.

Bracing himself against the upper companionway, with legs apart and head thrown back, he raised his resonant tenor above the howling wind and sang "Bonnie Mary of Argyle." Doble seemed entirely oblivious of the spray in his face and of the waves flooding across the deck and swirling and sucking at his seaboots, and he sang as he must have sung often before the most distinguished audiences.

Besotted youth that he was, the song stirred Tom's Scottish blood, and by the time Doble finished singing he was absolutely sober. His thoughts flew back to his childhood— the governor at Dean and church on Sundays; kind Mrs. Mitchell and her poor fowls; Joan and Dad at Liphook. Tom felt something warmer than rain wet his cheeks, and he stood for a long time in the wind and spray, pondering what life was all about.

By the time the little ship anchored outside the Pula harbor all was calm. Next morning the captain ordered everyone to eat a hearty breakfast, and Tom was hard put to keep up with the demand for fried eggs and bacon and toast. All those suffering from *mal de mer* had recovered, and the captain ordered, "All hands on deck!" Only those actively engaged in keeping the ship moving were allowed to stay below.

The crew lined the rails, gazing shoreward as the engines cut speed and the craft slowly maneuvered into position to begin its hazardous assignment.

Merely approaching the partially ruined town gave Tom a creepy feeling. As far as he could see, there was not even a dog left in Pula. Glassless windows in ruined buildings stared out to sea like sightless eye sockets. The wind moaned through tangles of broken power lines. Heaps of bricks and rubble blocked the narrow streets.

The harbor itself looked quite normal, and if the enemy followed its usual practice, the mines would be laid just under the surface of the sea, close to the jetty where ships berthed.

The crew members crowded the rail, watching, laughing, and talking about everything under the sun, except mines. It was nothing new to them to watch the steel cable from the boom sweep through the clear blue sea, its great toothed jaws ready to snap and release the submerged mines. They knew that when the freed mines surfaced, their own Royal Naval Patrol gunners stood ready to shoot them, and the mines would fill with water and sink, or else explode harmlessly in the sea.

The crew also knew that it was extremely dangerous work—especially the first time around. The ship circled slowly, and as it nosed closer and closer to the spot where the first mine was likely to be, they all strolled nonchalantly— still laughing and talking at the top of their voices—toward the bows where they would stand a better chance if the ship hit a mine and there was an explosion.

The first round took twenty-five eternity-long minutes, and Tom and his mates ignored one another's muffled sighs of relief when it ended without mishap and the doughty little craft moved in for a second sweep around the harbor. So far so good. Once more they steamed slowly around; the armlike cable clawed through the water, searching. Still no sign of a mine.

Again they steamed slowly around—and again. Four times, in tightening circles, they swept the harbor, watched by those silent, sightless windows in the ruined town. At last it was obvious that there were no mines.

But Intelligence said they were there, and Intelligence knew. The skipper decided to send a party of armed men ashore to search the town and quayside.

The crewmen saw them off with much cheering and chaffing:

"Don't bring back any wristwatches, Sandy."

"No silver vases or radios, mind!"

"Keep your hands off the bullion, Mac."

The search party laughed and waved back and gave the victory sign as their small boat moved off. They did not need to be reminded that the retreating enemy had probably laid booby traps, and if a man stooped to pick up some valuable exposed among the rubble, he would likely as not be killed or have his hand blown off or suffer other terrible injuries.

Through binoculars the crew watched the search party's progress along the nearer streets, but then they lost sight of them behind the ruined buildings, and those left on board could do nothing but hang over the rail smoking and yarning, waiting with ears atuned for the slightest sound of an explosion.

Nearly an hour later it came. The sound of a single shot close to the quay. The crew waited with nerves taut as steel cables until they saw the small boat returning. Anxiously they counted and recounted the men in the boat. As far as could be seen, the full complement of the search party was accounted for. Then what was the shot?

"It was Sandy shooting off the lock," Mac explained to Tom later. "We held our guns at the ready while we searched the town. Actually there's nothing much left at all. What hasn't been destroyed by bombs or taken away by the people when they evacuated has gone to looters. There wasn't a sign of a trip wire or a booby trap, and certainly no mines.

"We did everything over thoroughly until we came to an old building that looked like a warehouse. It was right at the end of the jetty and had a giant of a bolt and padlock fastening the door. Sandy shot off the padlock, and we gingerly pushed the door open. Sure enough, the mines were in there; all stacked neatly along the floor."

"What's the skipper going to do about them? Are we going to defuse them or something?"

"I don't know. I think he's relayed the find to headquarters and is waiting for orders."

He had indeed; and the orders came back that the ship was to return to base and leave the mines where they were. Apparently HQ thought the mines would not spoil by keeping. Tom's ship sailed back to Trieste, and before anything more was done, the news leaked out that a Yugoslav nationalist had crept back to the warehouse in Pula, set a fuse, and blown up the whole sixty mines.

The British Navy might have said, "Good riddance; it saved us the trouble" but for the fact that a ship was in port at the time, and many of the crew—along with local men, women, and children who had returned to their homes—were swimming in the harbor. The blast from the exploding mines blew their heads off.

The Allies lodged a strongly worded complaint, and the whole nasty episode threatened to flare up into an international incident until President Tito disclaimed all knowledge of the affair and promised that the offender would be tracked down and punished.

As well as clearing mines from specified areas where Intelligence knew they had been laid, the minesweepers cruised around searching for mines and saboteurs. When they located a mine the sweeping device cut it loose from its underwater moorings, and it bobbed to the surface to be shot down by the BYMS gunners. Their aim was to shoot a hole in the outer casing of the mine so that it slowly filled with water and sank to the bottom and finally corroded.

But it was a perilous pastime. If a gunner missed the

casing and hit one of the mine's projecting horns, the whole thing exploded—often taking the ship with it. Tom knew that more than one of the BYMS had gone to Davy Jones's locker that way. There was no second chance.

The skipper of Tom's ship lessened the risks by making sure that the ship and mine were as far apart as practicable before the gunners fired. If they missed outright, the shells ricocheted off the water and shot off into the blue distance, lost as far as the crew aboard were concerned. But sometimes even a lost shell carried death and danger with it, as Tom and his pals learned one afternoon.

"Missed it!" Tom slapped the ship's rail in mock applause. He and some of his mates crowded the side, watching the gunners shooting at a mine that had been swept up. Already three mines had been located, and after a series of missed shots, the gunners finally hit them and all three sank.

"Try again, Jack." Tom cupped his hands and shouted to the gunner. But again the shell missed its mark and whined off into the distance.

"Give it another go," Tom's mates joined in the jeering advice, but their shouts died away as they saw Sparks rush from his tiny wireless room and agitatedly rap on the captain's door.

Seconds later the captain strode to the bridge and barked orders that stopped both ship and gunners. The ship slowly backed up, and while the crew watched in silence, it swung around in a semicircle that took it to the opposite side of the floating mine.

"What's up?" Tom edged toward the nearest gunner, but the man on duty ignored him and thrust another shell into his gun. The captain waited until the mine was disposed of and then returned to his cabin.

Once he was out of sight, the word quickly spread around that all afternoon their gunners had been unwittingly shelling an onshore village. Unnoticed by the captain or anyone else on board, the mines they swept up had all been between the ship and the shore, and any shell that missed its mark whistled toward the unfortunate village.

There was no way the terrified villagers could contact the ship, and they cowered in their houses, expecting the worst every time a shell lobbed in their vicinity.

Finally the frantic village authorities telephoned their predicament to naval headquarters in Trieste. Headquarters easily identified and located the offending ship and radioed the situation to them.

Fortunately no one in the village was killed or injured, and the British Navy took care of any damages, but headquarters considered the incident was caused by carelessness on the part of the ship's officers. An inquiry was held, and the captain was severly censured.

"Too bad for the 'Old Man,' Tom grunted to Mac when the news leaked out. "It could've happened to anyone."

On another occasion when their ship was mine hunting around the Mediterranean, they had on board a scientist who was anxious to examine an unexploded sample of a new type German mine. He requested the skipper to bring one up for him.

When that news leaked out, there were a lot of rumblings below deck about "mad scientists willing to risk other people's necks," but when the time came that a mine was located, the crew were all on deck watching. Apparently the skipper felt equally as dubious about the project, for he also stayed on deck watching.

It was always a tense situation when the great mechanical claw of the minesweeper felt its way along the cable, clutched the chain of the underwater mine, and dragged it to the surface. Anything could go wrong.

Soon the freed mine bobbed gently about on the restless sea, and Tom wondered how it could be hauled up on deck without exploding. It was no featherweight. Besides the weight of the casing, chain, and all the interior mechanical devices, it contained about six hundred pounds of amatol, an explosive more powerful than pure TNT.

Obviously the ship's officers wondered the same thing

because Tom saw them conferring with the skipper while they leaned over the rail looking at the mine. Then a couple of the ship's divers went overboard and gingerly fastened a cable around the mine, and the ship's winch began to draw it out of the water.

At that point most of the crew abruptly decided to investigate the flying fish on the other side of the ship, but a sort of horrible fascination kept Tom there watching the instrument of death slowly ascending. He knew it only needed the slightest thing to go wrong. . . . What if the mine bumped hard against the side of the ship and triggered off an exploding device? What if the cable slipped as they were lowering the mine and one of the projections thumped the deck? They'd all be blown to smithereens. It was not a happy thought, and he unconsciously held his breath as he watched the awful thing rise.

Tom sensed that the fellows craning over the rail, too, and touching elbows with him on either side felt the same as he did. The whole atmosphere seemed as tense as the winching cable itself. Only the scientist, watching from the stern, looked to be at ease. Tom thought he probably did not realize the gravity of the situation.

Suddenly the skipper barked an order, and there was a concerted sigh of relief as the cable slackened and the mine slid safely back into the sea.

The skipper walked across to the scientist, and although Tom was not close enough to hear what he said, word quickly passed along that he had told the professor the risks were too great, and he was not going to jeopardize his ship and crew even in the cause of science. The gunners would dispose of the mine in the usual way.

The scientist looked downcast, but under his breath Tom gave three silent cheers for the "Old Man."

The small fleet of naval minesweepers did a big job in keeping the shipping lanes and harbors free of mines, but sometimes they missed one, and the results were tragic.

A couple of Allied ships had a close call right in Trieste's busy harbor. Even though the BYMS were certain that no saboteurs managed to lay mines without their knowledge, they made regular routine checks, and once when the three A's—*Ajax, Aurora, and Arethusa*—were in port, a routine check revealed four magnetic mines lurking near the quay.

When they were in Venice Tom's captain concentrated on the entrances to the long canals as being the most likely places for mines. He did not expect anyone to get past their defenses and mine further inside the canal. Consequently, one day an unfortunate little tug sailed right in, traversed a long canal, and edged into a welcoming berth, only to hit a mine and blow up, berth and all.

Later a troopship met a similar fate, with great loss of life, and those in charge of the BYMS learned to be even more careful of saboteurs.

Because of their ship's particular task, all the crewmen became mine conscious. They could spot mines at great distances. Once when Tom and a few of his mates had naval passes and were traveling to Rome for a couple of days' leave, he saw a mine in perfect position to blow up a train.

As the train rattled over a tall bridge spanning a narrow estuary, Tom leaned out of the window idly admiring the scenery and saw a mine bobbing corklike near one of the piers. It must have been laid at sea and come adrift. Tom's heart pounded, and he died a dozen deaths before the train reached the safety of the other side. Having no idea how to warn the Italian railway authorities, he only hoped that the mine would be discovered and removed before he made the return journey.

On that same leave, as Tom and his mates wandered around the streets of Rome, they fell into conversation with a couple of young fellows wearing civvies, who spoke passable English. The group went to the nearest café for a drink, and during their conversation, Tom discovered that the young fellows were deserters from the German side. Not only that but Tom's ship had cleared up the same mines that the German youths had helped to lay around Trieste and Venice.

The European part of the war was over, but around the Mediterranean, life was still terribly cheap. Fighting of one kind or another was commonplace. The Italians and the Yugoslavs were always at one another's throat, fighting in the streets over who should possess Trieste.

The Scots guards camped in the hills above the city, and often at night when the men were bored beyond endurance, a group of them sneaked out and scouted around in the dark until they came across a Yugoslav camp. Silent as shadows, they crept up and fired their guns into the camp and laughed themselves silly at the pandemonium they created.

A few nights later the performance was reversed. The Yugoslavs crept up to the Scots' camp, fired into their tents, and escaped into the darkness. Inevitably there were casualties on both sides, but that didn't stop the "fun."

These incidents were never recorded in official files or mentioned in newspaper reports, but they went on. Tom knew. He was there.

While Tom's ship was still based at Trieste, the men were assigned a new skipper. Charles Holbrook-Hook was a bull-necked, pompous sort of fellow who always smelled of whiskey and shaving soap, and who had the knack of rubbing people the wrong way at first meeting.

Tom was too junior—too far down the pecking scale—for the captain's peculiarities to bother him, but the senior crew and officers could not stand the man.

All the same, Tom shuddered along with the rest at the risks the new skipper took. When they were out on patrol and swept up a mine, the captain often took it into his head to shoot at the bobbing target with a Mauser pistol. At such close range it was a most sporting way of blowing up the ship—if he had been a good enough shot. He disregarded orders from headquarters, too, or interpreted them in a way that put his ship and crew in jeopardy. If the first lieutenant dared to make a suggestion, the skipper flared up and made all sorts of accusations, using the foulest language imaginable. Tom knew that the skipper gave the petty officers plenty of reason to hate him, but he had no idea how deep their resentment went—until one afternoon in Venice.

Tom was off duty and decided to go ashore for a while. A small fleet of rowboats always hung about the ship, and he clambered down into one of them and rowed in close to the harbor wall. At the Lido, the first open-air café he came to, he spied a group of fellows from his ship sitting at a table sipping drinks.

"Hi!" Tom stood up in the boat and waved to them, but instead of shouting back and beckoning to him to join them, they scowled in his direction, and Tom said to himself, "Oho, they've got a meet on. I know when I'm not welcome."

Turning around and rowing back to the ship, he persuaded Sparks to come ashore with him. They chose a different part of the harbor and drowned their troubles in beer at another quayside café.

For hours the two of them sat smoking, drinking, and talking. There was nothing better to do. Night fell, and the lights came on and shone out over the water. Tom always enjoyed watching them reflected on the restless sea. Sometimes they were long and narrow like iridescent serpents wriggling over the waves; sometimes, short and wide like beams from welcoming open windows.

Sparks grew drowsy and stopped talking. Tom leaned back in his chair with his feet on the table and listened to the waves slap-slapping against the harbor walls. He sniffed the briny breeze and thought about his Italian girl friends, how good the beer was at Romano's café, and what he'd do when he got back to Scotland.

For a long time he admired the lights and breathed in enough cool sea air to sober him a bit—enough to look at his watch and see how late the hour was. Sparks was asleep with his head on the table, almost in a plate of spaghetti. Tom shook him:

"Come on, shipmate. Time we were getting back."

Tom helped Sparks into the boat and rowed back to the

ship. He guided his mate to his bunk and then turned in himself. The next thing he knew someone had him by the shoulder, shining a flashlight in his face and shouting, "Get up on deck!"

Tom's thick tongue struggled to curse his tormentor, then his bleary eyes opened a crack, and he saw the gold braid and revolver. In an instant he leaped out of bed, pulled on his trousers, and raced for the deck.

Fellows seemed to be milling everywhere. Some of his own crew and some big chaps he quickly recognized as armed sailors from the Tank Landing-Craft anchored close by. In the middle of all the noise and confusion some of the petty officers battled to restrain a group of wild fellows, who shouted and waved fists and bottles as they tried to break free and get at the skipper. Charles Holbrook-Hook and "Jimmy the One"* were jammed up against the funnel. Their caps had been knocked off, and the deck around them was littered with potatoes and other missiles. A couple of the armed sailors stood ready to defend them.

Tom slunk back into the shadows. He did not need to be told that this was an ugly situation, and he did not want to be involved in something he knew nothing about. He edged his way to the outskirts of the crowd, but a burly sailor guarded the companionway. Oh, well, if he could not go below and sleep, at least he would keep as far as possible away from the trouble.

Looking around, Tom saw Sandy also skulking in the shadows and sidled up to him:

"What's it all about?"

"Unarmed mutiny," Sandy hissed. "Skipper accused the coxswain of stealing rum and filling the bottles up with pepper and water——"

" . . . and falsifying records." Doble was at Tom's elbow. "I've seen this coming. The cox'n's been getting madder and madder."

---

*Naval slang for any first lieutenant.

The three discussed the affair in hoarse whispers. To his dismay Tom found that Mac was deeply implicated. Poor, hotheaded Mac. This was one spot of trouble he'd not be able to talk his way out of.

Again Tom tried to slink back to his bunk, but huge sailors armed with tommy guns blocked the way. Yawning, he propped himself against the nearest solid object and settled down to wait. He could not put it into words, but he thanked his lucky stars that for once he was not involved in trouble.

Gradually the racket died down, and the guards got things sorted out. The apparent ringleaders were taken below, and the rest of the crew were hustled aboard the Tank Landing-Craft to spend the rest of the night under armed arrest.

"Regarded guilty until proved innocent," Doble grunted in Tom's ear, and Tom nodded, too weary to care about anything but a place to bunk down.

The next morning each member of the crew was called up separately and questioned. Tom and Sandy and Doble and most of the others were cleared and ordered to take the ship back to Trieste and report to headquarters. Tom enjoyed that part of it. With only a skeleton crew aboard, he had the responsibility of steering the ship all the way.

As soon as the ship reached Trieste it was put in quarantine. No one was allowed ashore until after the court-martial.

Even though Tom was cleared, he had to testify at the inquiry. They asked him a lot of questions. Was the captain popular? No. How do you know? Did you see or hear anything that made you suspect mutiny was afoot? Was there . . . ? Did you . . . ?

Day after day the questioning dragged on until at last sentence was pronounced on the ringleaders. The coxswain and MacDonald and five of the others received five-year prison sentences, and what was even worse—loss of seamanship papers. Tom groaned for them. All their years of training and experience gone—canceled out by one rash action. If they wanted a naval career when they came out of prison, they would have to begin all over again.

Other men who were less involved received lighter sentences, and Tom was among those completely exonerated.

By the time it was all over, the skipper was a changed man. The crew noticed how subdued he was; all the swank and bluster seemed to have disappeared, and he kept to himself as much as possible.

But the first lieutenant reacted differently. Digby was actually a fine fellow, and the crew regarded him highly. None of them disliked Jimmy the One; they knew he had to obey the skipper's mad orders the same as they did—only having the misfortune to be in authority, he suffered with the captain. But he did not seem to see it that way, and as the days passed he became moody, brooding over the disgrace.

Other sailors arrived to make up the ship's complement, and everything reverted to normal. Orders were received to go out on a new mission, and a few days before sailing, Tom had a night ashore.

Men on leave were expected to sign in before midnight, but it was a well-established custom that if a fellow did not make it aboard on time, one of his mates signed for him.

It was 12:30 AM by the time Tom reached the quayside, but he knew that Sandy, on watch, would have signed in for him, and he was not worried—until he saw the first lieutenant coming toward him.

Tom groaned. What rotten luck! But he'd better brave it out. "Good evening, sir." He stood aside to let the officer pass.

Digby did not reply. He seemed not to see or hear Tom but walked past, staring straight ahead, his eyes fixed and glassy.

Tom stared after him. Now what? Digby was a good sort, but that would not prevent him from doing his duty by latecomers.

Tom sneaked up the gangplank and sidled over to the watch. "Have you signed me in?"

"Yes, of course."

"That's done it! I've just passed Jimmy the One on the quayside."

"Oh, crumbs! Now we'll both be in for it!"

Tom shrugged. There was nothing they could do about it now. He crept below to his bunk.

After breakfast next morning Tom went on deck for his usual smoke and was just in time to see the skipper come on board.

"Huh," he sniffed to himself. "*He* can spend the whole night ashore with *his* girl friend, but *we* have to be in by midnight."

He watched idly as the captain let himself into his cabin. Minutes later he started in surprise when the skipper burst wildly out again, shouted to the coxswain about going for the provost martial, and dashed back down the gangplank.

Tom gaped after him. Was the captain crazy?

Less than twenty-four hours later the whole story leaked out. Digby had left his personal belongings and a suicide note in the captain's cabin. He could not stand the dishonor and scandal generated by the mutiny, it said, and he had decided to end it all.

The police traced him down the coast to Barcola, where he entered a swimming pool, put a .45 in his mouth, and blew his head off.

Months later Tom saw a report of his death in a London newspaper. No details were given. Digby was simply listed under "Battle Casualties."

The first lieutenant's suicide stirred up fresh animosity against the captain. The crew's murmurings finally came to the ears of headquarters, and they transferred Charles Holbrook-Hook to another ship.

Tom did not even see the new captain. His demobilization papers had come through, and he was running back and forth like a sand crab, packing his belongings and saying good-bye to his mates. Tom had joined the navy for hostilities only, and now that there was peace he was free to leave and go back to civilian life.

Tom went with a large company of "demobs" who journeyed overland to Britain; and, with them, he nearly went crazy when he set foot on English soil again. He had been away only for a couple of years. Some of the others had been gone a lot longer. Some even had been imprisoned or at the front and had despaired of ever making it back.

Every last one of them was in a mood to celebrate, and most of them made a concerted rush for the nearest pub, where they managed to drink themselves silly in the short time available before they boarded a train again; this time bound for Portland.

The men were so full of high spirits, literally and figuratively, that the petty officers gave up trying to control them and took themselves off to one of the other carriages for a card game.

That gave Tom a chance to show off. For no other reason than stupid bravado he opened the door of the moving train and let himself out onto the step. The icy wind tore at his clothes and threatened to blow him off, but he hung onto the guardrail and shouted and waved and made a great show of daring.

Tom's mates thought it a grand joke. To heighten the fun, they slammed the carriage door and locked it on the inside. Tom heard their roars of laughter above the clatter of the speeding wheels, and it urged him on to further buffoonery.

He clung on with hands only and kicked his legs out into space. He stood on the narrow step and let go with alternate hands, swinging out like a human pendulum. He did everything he could think of that would amuse his audience.

His mates crowded the windows and doors, grimacing at him through the glass, laughing and tapping on the pane to urge him on. But the joke began to wear thin as far as Tom was concerned. His feet numbed with cold. His hands cramped with the intensity of their grip on the iron rail. The train seemed to be going even faster; it rocked and swayed, and he could not keep his body pressed against the side.

With a thrill of terror he realized that he was in real danger. At any moment the train might come to a narrow bridge, and if his body swung out with the swaying of the carriage, then——

"Let me in," he yelled, trying to bang on the door with his head while he hung on desperately with both hands.

But his antics only brought a fresh round of applause. His mates thought it was all part of the act. Tom grew frantic with fear. The combination of wind and speed threatened to tear him loose at any moment. How much longer could his frozen hands grip the rail? After escaping all the perils of sea and war, was he to meet a miserable death in his own land, so near to his own home?

Sweat broke out all over him. Sober now, he cursed himself for his folly. What was he doing out here anyway?

Again and again Tom thumped the door with his head. He tried to raise his foot to kick at it but nearly lost his balance. One of his mates threw open the glass portion of the door and leaned out to jeer at him. Tom lunged toward him, and as the fellow instinctively drew back, Tom thrust his head through the opening. Before the fellow could slam the pane shut, Tom made a superhuman effort and pulled himself through to collapse, shaking, on the floor.

His head was bleeding—but he was safe. For minutes he lay there panting. The sight of his strained face sobered his companions, and he heard one of them muttering, "He could have been killed."

All the laughter and high spirits faded into the night, and the rest of the journey passed uneventfully.

Once in Portland it did not take too long to complete all the formalities and get home to Liphook. Tom found that his dad had retired from the army; sister Joan and Aunt Julie had returned to London, George came and went. Things were the same, yet different.

For about six months Tom hung around the old town, smoking and drinking, flirting with the girls, watching his accumulated pay disappear like an ebbing tide.

Once or twice his dad suggested that Tom ought to make plans for the future—settle down, decide on a career of some sort. Tom nodded. He knew the old man was right, but he was only twenty and the future seemed far, far away. He was having a lot of fun in the present, and he liked it that way.

But when his money was all gone Tom had to spend more time sober, and he soon became restless. There were plenty of jobs available, but he could not imagine himself tied up in an office. Mining or farming did not appeal to him either, and he was not educated for anything else. He loved the sea, and he could always rejoin the navy, but now that he was free of that, he was not sure that he wanted to go back.

Once again it was George who led the way. He had been demobilized a short while before Tom, and after only a few weeks at home he joined NAAFI, the Navy, Army, and Air Force Institute that handled canteen supplies. George worked aboard the battleship King George V, and he seemed to be having a great time.

His enthusiasm for the job infected Tom, and he decided to join NAAFI too. He did not make it to the King George V with George but was assigned to a medium cruiser, the Sirius.

Once aboard, Tom quickly stowed his belongings on the messdeck and raced up on deck. Yo-ho, it was good to be at sea again, even though their first cruise was only across the channel to Antwerp in Belgium. He paced the deck, rapidly regaining his sea legs, breathing in great lungfuls of salty air. Yes, this was the life; being a landlubber did not suit him.

Nonetheless, the Sirius had scarcely tied up in Antwerp before Tom and a gang of his new friends raced down the gangplank and off to the nearest bar to try the Belgian beer. They found it equally as potent as its British counterpart, and late at night they staggered back to the ship.

Belgian officials guarded the wharf gates, and the sailors were expected to show their ship passes before they were allowed through. Tom's companions showed their passes and went through, but Tom could not find his.

He searched through pocket and wallet and cap. He even took off his shoes and shook them out in a befuddled sort of hope that he might have put it in a shoe for safekeeping. No pass. He must have lost it at one of the bars they visited, but he had not the vaguest idea which one. He would have to try and bluff his way back to the ship without it.

Tom drew himself up and tried to appear erect and reasonably sober as he approached the gate and explained to the official that he had lost his pass. But the guard understood very little English, and he only stared blankly at him.

Tom's new mates stood a little way inside the gate enjoying his predicament, and he appealed to them:

"Come on, fellows, tell him who I am. Tell him I belong on the same ship as you do. Tell him the NAFFI employees always wear civvies."

The guard caught on to what Tom was saying and beckoned the other fellows over. "Is he—belong—your—ship?"

As one man the fellows straightened their faces and shook their heads. "Never saw him before."

Tom swore at them and shouted that they were liars, but he was helpless. Without a pass the guards would not let him through, and if these fellows walked off and left him . . . "Aw, come on, fellows," he pleaded. "Tell him I'm with you."

At length they could keep their faces straight no longer, and their boisterous laughter gave them away. The official did not understand it all, but he realized some sort of tomfoolery was afoot, and he let Tom through the gate.

For some time the Sirius cruised up and down the coasts of Europe before returning to Portsmouth. Tom was well satisfied with his canteen job. He was the only one in the canteen besides "Corky," the manager, who did all the buying and checking of stores. The canteen carried a big variety of items, some that civilians rarely saw even though the war was a year in the past. The stuff was cheap, too, much cheaper than it could be purchased ashore, and Tom always made sure that his pockets were filled when he went on leave.

One afternoon both he and Corky were going ashore, and just before they locked up, the manager swung around to Tom:

"Aren't you taking anything ashore, Tom?"

For a moment Tom was speechless. He knew that Corky

had a reputation for being "the biggest rogue unhung," and the unexpected question confused him.

"I've got a few packets of cigs in my pockets," he admitted. "I'd be afraid of being caught if I took more than that."

"No worries," Corky assured him. "You'll be OK. Make up a parcel and come with me."

Still dubious, Tom stuffed a thick paper sack with cartons of cigarettes and bars of chocolate and followed his boss up on deck.

Corky carried two bulging sacks and a big green suitcase. Tom knew that all three containers were stuffed with contraband, and he wondered how Corky could get away with such doings. They started down the gangplank, and Corky edged close to Tom and whispered.

"Just walk straight ahead and out the gates. They won't stop you when they see that you're with me."

Tom wished he felt as confident as Corky did, but the manager pushed him ahead, and there was nothing he could do but stumble on toward the gate with pounding heart and with legs that felt like jelly. The officers were staring hard at the sack he carried. What had he let himself in for now?

Instead of following Tom, Corky made straight for the shed that served as dockyard police office and disappeared inside. At the same instant both of the officers at the gate turned their backs and examined the wall behind them while Tom walked through unchallenged.

"Phew!" Tom puffed his relief. He did not stop walking until a corner of the building hid him from view. A few minutes later Corky joined him there, and Tom noticed that one of the paper sacks was missing.

"Righto, shipmate," Corky winked. "Let's go."

That was only the beginning. The canteen manager and his assistant made a lot of money out of their illicit trading. On board ship cigarettes sold for eight cents a packet, while ashore the blackmarket brought forty cents. Wine and spirits, hams, canned foods, and all kinds of other goodies were in similar ratio, and what Corky and Tom did not smuggle ashore for their families, they sold on the "black."

By the time Tom was promoted to being a canteen manager himself, he had become an expert. In every port he found at least one corrupt official—customs or police—who would accept a "gift." Tom only had to lay low and make cautious inquiries until he found the right one.

Although Tom considered himself a success, he never tried anything as bold as the ruse Corky told him about. A fellow who managed the canteen on another NAAFI ship went down the gangplank one day carrying his big, green, navy-issue suitcase, and the customs official stopped him at the gate.

"What's in the suitcase, Jack?"

"The skipper's cat. I've got to take it to his house for him."

"Ho, ho. That's a likely one. Open it up, Jack."

"It *is* a cat, I tell you. It will get away if I open the suitcase."

"Open it anyway."

The canteen manager angrily wrenched the lid up and a huge cat sprang out and raced back along the dockside and up the gangplank.

"See! I told you it was a cat. Now I'll have to go back and catch the so-and-so animal again."

"Sorry, Jack."

Muttering indignantly, the manager went back to the ship and nearly an hour later reappeared at the exit carrying his big, green suitcase.

"Well," he sputtered. "I caught it at last. Do you want me to open the suitcase again?"

"No, Jack, we'll let it go." The customs officer waved him through, and the manager with his contraband-loaded case went on his way.

On board ship Tom's mates knew what went on, or if they did not know they guessed, and they envied him his luck. Most of them openly said that they would do the same if they had his position; a few warned him that he would push his luck too far.

"You'll be caught one day. You see if you're not."

Tom thought their predictions had come true on one occasion when his ship put into Portland. As soon as they berthed, the customs officers came on board and asked for the canteen manager.

"He's below in the canteen." One of Tom's friends directed the customs men and then doubled back to tell the others that Tom was about to be arrested. A dozen or so of them sneaked up to the back of the canteen so as not to miss the fun, and while the officers inside made their check, Tom could hear his mates outside snickering and whispering, "They've caught him at last. Poor old Tom. He had it coming."

Their chuckles did not do anything for Tom's peace of mind, and he hoped that the customs officials were stone-deaf. Mentally chewing his fingernails, he stood aside until the men finished their checking and said that everything was in order, then he moved forward to usher them out and lock the door. But one of the customs men stopped him.

"We'd like to buy a few things, Jack."

Tom's heart plummeted to his boots. Now he was in a fix. If he let them buy a whack of duty-free stuff, they could then turn around and charge him with dishonest practices, and he would be in trouble. On the other hand, if he acted all honest and refused to let them have anything, they could make life very difficult for him—and not only in Portland. That sort of word gets around, and he'd be a marked man in every port.

What should he do? His whirling thoughts halted, and he decided to take a chance.

"How much do you want?"

"Oh, just a couple of hams for Christmas, Jack, and a few cartons of cigarettes."

Tom sold them what they asked for, and they, in turn, told him to fill up his big, green suitcase and they'd give him a lift ashore in the customs launch. He accepted the offer. At the customshouse steps they shook hands and parted, and to Tom's great relief that was the last he ever heard of the incident.

While they were in Portland Tom's ship put into the floating dock for repairs. This was a new experience for Tom and many of the other sailors. They became adept at climbing up and down the sixty-foot iron ladder on the side of the dock, balancing on the breakwater, and letting themselves down into the little trot-boat that took them to and from shore.

One early morning Tom ignored the falling barometer and decided to spend his day off ashore. By ten o'clock that night he knew he had made the wrong decision.

Even in the shelter of Portland harbor a howling North Atlantic gale whipped the sea into mountainous waves, and Tom knew he would have trouble getting back to his ship. Cowering miserably at the edge of the pier, he turned up his coat collar and wondered whether his day ashore had been worth it. Oh, it had been cozy enough in the public house saloon, drinking and smoking with his buddies, playing cards and joking with sailors from other ships; but now——

Narrowing his eyes to keep out the driving rain, he searched the darkness for the faint glimmer of the trot-boat navigation lights and cursed his bad luck. Why had it turned out such foul weather? He knew very well that the skipper of the little boat that plied between the ships and shore would not want to risk his frail craft being smashed like eggshell against the thick steel breakwater of the floating dock where Tom's ship was shored up.

In a brief lull in the gale Tom heard the throb of the trot-boat engine and the skipper's shout, "Where to, Jack?"

Tom cupped his hands to his mouth and shouted the name of his ship: "*Helmsdale*, she's in the floating dock."

"Very risky," the skipper yelled back, while he tried to hold his craft for Tom to jump in. "Why don't you sleep on one of the battleships?"

"Aw, Jack, I'd rather sleep in my own bunk."

Tom scrambled aboard and crouched in the bottom of the boat with a couple of other sailors returning from shore leave. The noise of crashing seas and whistling wind made conversation impossible, and they huddled wretchedly together, with the salt spray stinging their cold faces and chapped hands.

Occasionally the bouncing navigation lights picked out the black shapes of mighty ships straining at their anchors; and once or twice the little trot-boat slowed down, its engine fighting fiercely against the pounding waves, while a sailor leaped out and grasped the lowest rung of the iron ladder that led him upward to the safety of his home ship.

When only Tom was left he lurched forward to where the skipper, his shiny oilskins gleaming in the faint light, stood at the wheel, and strained his eyes to make out the lights of his ship. Surely they must be getting close to the floating dock. Yes, there it was, running seas dashing against its heavy breakwater and sending showers of spray skyward.

"I'll go in as close as I dare," the skipper yelled above the storm. "Then you'll have to jump for it."

Tom nodded automatically and climbed onto the gun-wale, balancing precariously as the tiny boat bucked and rocked. He drew his greatcoat tightly around him and tensed for the spring.

"When I say, 'Right,' you jump." Fighting the waves, the skipper inched as close to the dock's breakwater as he dared and shouted, "Right!"

Tom let go of the rail and jumped—at the same instant as a mountainous wave tossed the light craft aside. He missed the edge of the breakwater and hurtled onto the steel bottom of the dock, landing on his face only a handbreadth from a heavy iron ringbolt that protruded nearly twelve inches into the air.

Half-stunned, cut and bleeding, Tom heard a voice, faint and far off, call, "Are you all right, Jack?"

"Right!" he shouted back, his already swollen lips scarcely shaping the word. Above the pounding seas he heard the trot-boat chug away.

Muttering thickly, Tom picked himself up. He moved each arm and leg carefully. No bones seemed to be broken, but blood trickled from his head onto his torn clothing.

Still half-drunk, battered and dazed, he stared stupidly at

the iron ringbolt barely discernible in the faint arc of light from the ship's prow far above. Tom shivered and cursed aloud. A few inches to the right, and he——

Still cursing, he staggered dizzily to the perpendicular iron ladder leading up to the catwalk on the dockside. Ordinarily he went up and down the sixty-foot ladder like a monkey. Now, waiting until his head cleared sufficiently to begin the climb, he clung to the lower rungs.

His arms and legs seemed like lead. His head felt as large as a monument and heavy as a cannonball. Every roll and sway of the dock threatened to pitch him down, but he clung on, each desperate step more painful than the last.

Reaching the top, he tottered across the gangplank to the ship's deck, swearing at the top of his voice. He passed the skipper's cabin just as the captain's wife came out the door.

The startled woman took one look at him and backed inside. Moments later the skipper appeared and followed the blood trail to where Tom sagged against the ship's rail.

"What happened, sailor?"

Struggling to come to attention, Tom blurted, "I fell into the dock, sir."

The skipper stared at him; apparently deciding that Tom told the truth, he called a petty officer to assess the junior's injuries and take him ashore to the naval medical officer.

By the time the ship's boat was launched and had braved the stormy sea back to the shore, the doctor assigned to the casualty department of the naval sick bay had gone off duty.

A couple of orderlies, disgruntled at having their card game disturbed, hustled Tom into a bare, white room, yanked off his coat, and told him to lie down on a bench while they swabbed the caked blood off his face and head.

"How'd you get into this mess? Been fighting?"

"No." In brief, painful words Tom explained his accident.

"You're lucky you didn't bash your brains out, Jack." One of the orderlies attacked Tom's blood-matted hair with a razor blade.

"Are you sure he had any?" joked the other. "Anyone

who'd try a jump like that on a night like this——"

Tom did not reply.

The first orderly poured acriflavine generously into Tom's wounds. "By rights you oughta have a coupla stitches there, and there." He poked none too gently at Tom's forehead.

Tom tried not to give them the satisfaction of seeing him flinch, and only cursed under his breath as the fiery liquid burned into his gaping cuts.

"It'll be too late for stitching tomorrow, but you'd better come back and let the quack decide what to do for you."

"Not likely," Tom muttered, and the orderly laughed and drew the wound edges together with adhesive tape.

"You'll be OK, Jack. Just don't wash your face for a while."

Tom slid stiffly from the bench, climbed into his greatcoat, and for the third time that night, in the wildest weather he had ever known in port, made a safe voyage through the storm.

Officially the war was over, but the British Navy still spent a lot of time and money developing new weapons, perfecting old ones, and experimenting with different safety devices.

Tom's next assignment with NAAFI was on an experimental ship plying between the south of England and the coasts of Gibraltar. On this particular voyage the navy tested an antisubmarine defense nicknamed The Nightshirt.

The exact nature of the device was a closely guarded secret, but as far as Tom could see, it consisted of a tubular framework with thousands of little holes in it. This was attached aft under water, creating a system of bubbles to foil the enemy's sonar equipment. Tom never found out whether the powers that be were satisfied with the device, but he liked to hang over the stern rail when he was off duty and watch the myriads of bubbles, foaming and frothing and bursting in the ship's wake.

Then there was a listening device, a dome-shaped attachment fastened like a giant blister underneath the ship. It was supposed to pick up the sounds of submarine activity. It worked well, too. The crew often amused themselves listening to fish noises amplified from the ocean depths.

There were usually enough duties to keep the crewmen busy by day, but at night the frosty stars twinkled from a moonless sky, and Tom and his pals mooched around the deck, aimless and bored. They had sung all their ribald songs and told all the risqué jokes and played cards until they were tired of them. What else was there to do on a ship miles out to sea?

The irrepressible Tom did not remain bored for long. One night as they leaned over the rail, watching the ship's wake gleaming palely in the starlight, he nudged a pal, Long Len.

"Tell you what, Long, let's have some fun with the officers."

"How?"

"See this?" Tom pulled a peashooter out of his pocket. "Bought it for a lark last time I was on shore leave. Had a hunch it might come in handy."

"What are you going to do with it?"

"Have some fun." Tom felt in another pocket and brought out a handful of dried peas. "Helped myself to these last time I was in the galley."

Long Len guffawed, and two or three of the other fellows strolling the deck halted and looked in their direction. Tom beckoned them over and rapidly outlined his plan.

"Come along the deck a bit. Right. The porthole of the officer's mess is directly below, and you can see the light shining out over the sea. Now I want a couple of you fellows to hold my ankles and lower me over the side, and I'll go down headfirst and shoot at those fine fellows while they're eating. They'll wonder what's hit them."

"What fun!" Len chortled, and the other fellows slapped Tom on the back and told him that he was a genius.

"Give that scientist one from me," Long Len begged. "He's a pain, that fellow."

Tom, slipping his boots off so the fellows could get a better grip on his ankles, climbed over the rail and stood poised on the other side, holding tightly to one of the stanchions. "Now you pull me back up as soon as I wave my hand," he directed.

"I don't want those SNOs catching me."

"Righto!"

"Off you go, Tom."

Long Len and Stan each took one of Tom's ankles with both hands and braced themselves against the ship's roll, while Harry leaned over the rail and reported Tom's progress.

"He's right at the porthole now. He's taking aim; keep him as steady as you can. Wow, he's sent half a dozen through—I saw them against the light. Quick! Quick! He's signaling to be pulled up!"

Puffing and panting, the fellows dragged a red-faced Tom back to the deck and under the rail ropes, then all of them collapsed in a helpless, chuckling heap.

"You should—have seen Jimmy—the One——" Tom rocked with subdued laughter. "I got him a beauty on the side of his face. He rubbed his cheek and looked around to see what had stung him. I got the scientist, too, Len, on the back of his neck. He spluttered into his soup and swung around as if one of the stewards had stabbed him from behind."

"Do you think they saw you?"

"Nope. The rest of the shots went wide. Just as long as they don't find the peas lying round anywhere, they won't suspect anything."

"I'd have given anything to see their faces!" Stan rolled on the deck holding his aching sides. "Do it again tomorrow night, Tom."

"No," Long Len spoke up, "Once is enough. If anything happened and we lost our grip, it'd be curtains for Tom."

"Aw, what could happen?" Tom scoffed. "I can swim."

All the same, a swift vision of the ship's churning propellers flashed into his mind, and he let the matter drop.

None of the other fellows volunteered for the dangerous sport, and henceforth the officers dined in peace.

Tom's last and longest voyage with NAAFI was to South Africa aboard the *Cape Town Castle*. Someone was needed to manage the stores on the naval destroyer *Kempenfelt*, and when the position was offered to Tom he jumped at the chance of leaving foggy old England.

He found the work aboard the *Kempenfelt* most agreeable, the crew were pleasant fellows and easy to get along with, and South Africa was another of those palmy, balmy places he used to dream about. He loved it at first sight.

One afternoon Tom went ashore. He wandered aimlessly around the streets of Simonstown, admiring the flowering shrubs and well-kept lawns; basking in the sunshine's mellow warmth; enjoying a general feeling of well-being. His footsteps led toward the center of town, where many people were coming and going.

A neatly dressed man about thirty years old stopped him and asked, "Are you a Christian?"

The approach flabbergasted Tom. He was used to being asked for a match or directions to a street or even a "touch" to buy a cup of coffee; but, "Are you a Christian?" The cheek of the fellow!

"Yes, of course I am." Tom's face flushed. He was free, white, and a British subject. That made him a Christian, didn't it?

The stranger thrust a paper toward him. "Good, then I want you to know that Jesus Christ is about to set up His new kingdom. This paper tells all about it." Talking very fast, he pushed the paper into Tom's hand. To his surprise Tom found himself reaching into his wallet and paying the amount the man asked for.

"Do you read the Bible?"

Tom admitted that he didn't even own a Bible, and the stranger reached into his attaché case and brought out a new Bible. "You must have a Bible. You can't be a Christian without a Bible."

Slightly dazed by the barrage of words, Tom bought that too.

They talked for a long time. The stranger was a friendly sort and did most of the talking, but they exchanged names and addresses, and the man urged Tom to visit him whenever the *Kempenfelt* was in Simonstown. Then he gave Tom a hearty slap on the back and swung off down the street with, "So long, Tom. I've got to get on with the King's business."

Tom waved halfheartedly and turned his attention to the book and paper. How on earth had he gotten himself into this? What would the fellows say? He strolled along with his hands behind his back until he neared the ship and saw a few of the crew lining the rail, idly watching those on leave coming and going.

Quickly Tom stuffed the Bible under his jacket and folded his arm across his chest. The paper fitted perfectly into his pocket, and he smuggled them both aboard without the fellows seeing them.

As soon as he reached his cabin Tom hid the Bible in the bottom of his seabag. He leafed through the paper, but saw nothing that caught his attention. He crumpled it up and threw it out the porthole.

Early one morning, a few weeks after his conversation with the man in Simonstown, Tom leaned over the ship's rail, smoking his usual "coffin nails" before he began work in the canteen. Suddenly feeling an inexplicable urge to quit, he pulled the half-smoked cigarette out of his mouth and looked at it.

"You're not doing me any good," he said, flinging it into the sea.

Astounded by what he had done, he stepped back, half-expecting to be stricken by some terrible, tearing torment. Conditioned by the tales other fellows told of the agonies they suffered when trying to quit to please mother or girl friend, Tom was amazed when day followed day, and he had no headache, no chest pains, and no further desire to smoke. In fact, he felt just fine, and very pleased and proud of himself.

About a month later one of Tom's pals offered him a cigarette, and to test himself, Tom took it and smoked it down to the butt. It left his throat dry and burning, and he never touched another.

PART FOUR

The Taming of Thomas

"I think I'll stay on in South Africa." Tom made the decision one beautiful morning when the sun sparkled and shimmered over the shining sea and the warm breeze fanned his sun-tanned cheeks. It was March, 1951. His contract with NAAFI was about to expire, and he must decide whether or not he wanted to return to England.

Tom remembered the cold and snow in Edinburgh, and the fogs and icy winds in Portland. No, this climate was more to his liking. Besides, George and Joan were both married now and would not want him butting in. Dad was getting on—but he was comfortably settled in Liphook. No, he was not needed at home. He'd be much better off to begin a new life for himself out here.

Tom left his ship in Simonstown, and it did not take him long to find an office job with the London and Lancashire Insurance Company in Saint George's Street, Cape Town, and a place to stay with Mrs. Holtrop in the suburb of Claremont.

Tom, still young enough at twenty-four to adapt to a new way of life, soon settled down to being a landlubber. He enjoyed his work, and except for Mrs. Prins, the rest of the office staff were fellows and girls about his own age.

Mrs. Prins, much older than the rest of them, was a very religious person, always talking about God and telling the staff things that were written in the Bible. They put up with her doses of religion because she was so kind and sweet in other ways. In fact, they had a lot of fun at Mrs. Prins's expense and teased her unmercifully. In particular, Tom found it hilariously funny that she tried to reform a wild fellow like him.

"Don't you worry about me, Mrs. Prins," he'd say. "I can't imagine myself playing a harp anyway. And I really enjoy the heat, you know. That's why I'm staying on in Africa. Hellfire will probably only be comfortable for me." He winked at the others. A wave of titters rolled around the office, and kind Mrs. Prins smiled her patient smile.

Month after month passed, all following the same pattern of pleasant living. In fine weather Tom formed the habit of strolling off by himself at noon and eating his lunch in the Botanical Gardens. He enjoyed the fresh air after the stuffy office atmosphere, and he never seemed able to get enough of the glorious sunshine.

Tom's happy-go-lucky personality made him an easy mixer. He was popular with most people, and his life was punctuated by a succession of romances, some more serious than others. Pat, his current girl friend, had two brothers who were keen spear fishers, and as enthusiasts do, one Sunday they urged Tom to join them in the sport.

"We can borrow a snorkel and mask for you, Tom. You ought to try the game. You'll be hooked."

"I thought it was fish you hooked," Tom quipped.

Jim made a face at him. "No, smarty, we spear them."

"Okay, then, I'll try it. Where do you go?"

"To Smitswinkel Bay, near Cape Point. It's a fine place. Plenty of rocks for the fish to hide in."

Sunday found the three young men in swim shorts, unloading their gear on the bay shore about thirty miles from Camp Town. Bright sunlight reflected off the sparkling sea, a stiff breeze churned up little pockets of loose sand, and a high surf pounding against the rocks showered veils of white spray high into the air.

Tom paused to admire the scene and savor the salt spray on his face. His old love for the sea surged through him , and for a moment he forgot that he was an office-bound landlubber. Bob's words jolted him back to reality.

"It's a bit choppy today, but it'll be all right once we get deep enough."

"A bit choppy—that's an understatement," thought Tom. "And I don't like the looks of those rocks. A fellow could be dashed in pieces."

Tom's sea experiences had been mostly aboard ship, and he did not feel quite so much at home in the briny depths, but there was no turning back now. Bob was at his side, putting the snorkel tube into his mouth, adjusting his mask.

"Follow us," he shouted in Tom's ear and then loped off to join his brother, who was already lowering himself into the sea.

Tom picked his way gingerly over the rocks and let himself down as Jim and Bob had done. Deep water closed over his head. He began to swim.

About a hundred yards out from shore a mighty wave caught him side-on, twisting his mask and tearing it off his face. The air tube rotated in his mouth, ripping his gums.

Tom cried out in pain, and half the Atlantic Ocean poured down his throat. It all happened so fast, so unexpectedly, that he panicked. Tons of water pressed down on him. He fought to find the surface—to grasp something—but there was nothing. He kicked and struggled but sank deeper. Blackness closed around him.

"Steady, Tom, steady. Use your head." As clearly as words the impression came, and Tom relaxed. He let the swelling bear him upward—it seemed to take years. He thought his lungs would explode. The wave rushed shoreward.

For an instant his head cleared the water—he took a great gulp of air. The rocks cut and scraped his flesh as the wave threw him high onto their treacherous surface. His clutching, desperate fingers closed around a rough projection, and he clung to it as the receding waters tried to suck him back to their greedy depths.

From some unknown reservoir Tom summoned enough strength to crawl out of reach of the churning sea, and he sprawled there, gasping and coughing, while the benign sun warmed his chilled body.

"You're lucky to be alive, Tom." It was Mrs. Prins's gentle voice speaking. News of his narrow escape had leaked out, and the whole office buzzed with the story.

"Have you ever thought what would have happened if you'd drowned, Tom?"

"Oh, I suppose my soul would've flitted off to heaven," Tom laughed lightly and took up his pen.

"But what about the judgment, Tom?"

"Well, what about it?"

Tom liked nothing better than to lead Mrs. Prins into one of her ever-ready religious talks so that he could tease her and amuse the listening office personnel.

"It's a very important event, Tom." Mrs. Prins looked at the clock. "It will soon be closing time. If you can wait awhile after work I'll show you from the Bible where——"

"Sorry, not today. I have a very important engagement this afternoon." Tom winked at the others, bending over their desks to hide their mirth. "Some other time, Mrs. P. Some other time."

One lunch hour Tom sat in his usual place at the gardens, munching his sandwiches; they tasted dry and flavorless and seemed to stick in his throat. His head ached too, and when he stopped to analyze it, he decided that he felt rather strange all over. He had not been sitting in the sun long enough to have a sunstroke. Perhaps he was coming down with the flu—there was a lot of it about.

Tom threw the rest of his lunch to the birds and managed to smile as he watched them fluttering and fighting over tidbits. He stretched out on the cool green grass and dozed for a while. But when it came time to return to the office he felt no better. Instead he felt distinctly worse. His head really throbbed now, and his body ached all over. Groggily he pulled himself up and staggered to the nearest telephone booth.

"Is that you, Pat? It's Tom here. I'm in the gardens, but I've suddenly taken ill. I'll have to go home. S'pose it's flu. Ring the office for me, will you?"

Somehow Tom made his way to the train and out to his lodgings in Claremont. In a blur of aches and pains and rising fever he struggled out of his clothes and flopped into bed.

"Don't want any supper," he said thickly when his landlady called him to eat.

"Don't want any breakfast," he groaned next morning when she called him for work.

That good lady became worried, and ignoring Tom's protests, called a doctor who examined him and packed him straight off to the Groote Schuur.

"I think you've got diptheria, my lad, and hospital's the only place for you."

By the time Tom was installed in a hospital bed he was too sick to care what happened to him. He scarcely noticed the blood tests and throat swabs and all the other tests that finally resulted in his illness being diagnosed as glandular fever.

Once he was vaguely aware that the doctor and a crowd of students were around his bed, all staring solemnly at him while the doctor described his symptoms and told them to make a diagnosis.

Days passed, each one more miserable that the last, until gradually his fever responded to treatment and Tom began the long, slow road to recovery.

As soon as he began to improve, some of the fellows from the office visited him and brought him greetings from Mrs. Prins and a book she had sent.

"She said to tell you that she's sorry she can't come to see you, Tom, but she lives too far away. She sent you a book to read."

Joe tossed it onto the bedcover, and Tom picked the book up and read aloud its title, *God's Way Out*.

"Typical of Mrs. P.," he grinned, and Joe shrugged and turned the conversation to other topics.

Tom's interest in religion still registered at zero, but for want of something better to do, he read the book. It was not too bad at all. In fact, he grudgingly admitted to himself, parts of it were quite interesting.

The next time Joe came to visit he carried another message from Mrs. Prins. "She said she's enrolled you in a free Bible correspondence course, Tom. She says it will give you something to do during your convalescence."

"She might be right at that," Tom grunted. "The days seem awfully long."

A few days later the Bible lessons arrived. Tom read the first ones through, and after a little thought, penciled in the answers. He had expected the lessons to be dry and ponderous, akin to the Sunday sermons he remembered from his boyhood at Dean. Instead he found some parts of them quite interesting, and more than once he commented to himself, "Well, whaddya know! Fancy the Bible saying that."

One particular lesson in the Bible course caught Tom's attention. It was called "The State of the Dead." When he first read the title his thoughts flew to Mrs. Barnes at Dean, and all his old horror of death surfaced. Shuddering, he tossed the leaflet aside and concentrated on the other lessons.

One by one he read them, laboriously checked the answers, and filled in the question papers. When they were finished and mailed he reluctantly picked up "The State of the Dead." He'd have to do this one, too, or Mrs. Prins would want to know why.

As Tom read the leaflet, his hostility melted. It said in John 11:11-14 that Jesus spoke of death as a sleep. And texts in Ecclesiastes 9:5, 6 and Job 14:21 proved that dead people know nothing of what goes on in this world. When people die they do not go to either heaven or hell. Ecclesiastes 3:20 says they go to the grave and return to dust.

When Jesus comes back to earth He will reward everyone according to his works (Matthew 16:27; Revelation 22:12).

There were a lot more references, but Tom was satisfied. He lay back on his pillow and thought of all the tales of ghosts coming back and haunting people. He shook his head. "Nope, this makes sense. The dead can't harm anyone because they're asleep in their graves.''

He felt strangely comforted by this discovery and never doubted the truth of it.

During his stay in the hospital Tom became friendly with a number of the nurses. They were a great bunch of people, all of them. Particularly George Schoonraad.

No matter what happened, George remained unruffled. Regardless of how demanding or unreasonable a patient might be, George treated him kindly and pleasantly. In an odd sort of way the male nurse reminded Tom of Mrs. Prins.

On the rare occasions when Nurse George had a few spare minutes he came to Tom's bedside and inquired about the Bible lessons. "How are they going today, Tom?"

"Aw, not bad. I can't seem to find the answer to question 8, though."

"Let me have a look."

George took the leaflet and read it aloud, paraphrasing the difficult part to make it easier for Tom to understand.

"You really need a Bible, Tom. There are a lot more texts about the subject than the ones printed in these leaflets."

"As a matter of fact I have one back at my 'digs.' Fellow on the street in Simonstown sold it to me."

"Get someone to bring it in for you. I'm sure you'll find it helpful."

A bell rang, and George had to go answer it, but Tom acted on his suggestion, and when his Bible was brought in he began to read it.

Used as he was to reading novels, he began at the first page and read about Creation; the story of Adam and Eve; Cain and Abel; Noah's Flood. All of these were vaguely familiar. But when he reached Genesis 10 and 11 and bogged down in the "begats," Tom became irritated. "Who cares who begat who?" He leafed angrily through the pages, reading a little here and there until he came to the New Testament. That was not so bad, and every day after he completed his Bible lesson, he read a little of the Bible. But it really did not hold his interest, and he nearly always yawned himself to sleep in the middle of a verse.

By the time Tom was well enough to leave the hospital, he was back to normal in every way. His first act on returning to his lodgings was to cram the Bible back into the bottom of his seabag, and his second act was to go to the nearest hotel for a drink.

"Boy, nobody knows how I've been longing for a beer," he muttered to himself as he blew the froth off his first mug.

One drink followed another, and in no time at all Tom was beyond the stage of being merry—he was rolling drunk. Perhaps his forced abstinence in the hospital had made his stomach more sensitive. At any rate inside of two hours he staggered back to his room with a sack of bottles under his arm, and during the next few days he went on a bender to end all benders.

It did too. When Tom finally sobered enough to become conscious of his throbbing head and the nausea of his heaving stomach, he quit. Quit cold.

Never again did he drink himself silly. He decided, as he had with tobacco, that alcohol was doing him no good.

"I'm off the booze," he told his mates a week or two later when he returned to work, and neither their raucous laughter or the quiet gleam of triumph in Mrs. Prin's eyes disturbed him.

"How did you enjoy the Bible lessons, Tom?" she asked.

"Oh, not bad. Filled in the time anyway."

"There're some evangelistic meetings on over your way," she said. "A couple of American evangelists named Hassenpflug and Turner have pitched a big tent in Claremont. You ought to go along and hear them speak."

"False prophets," Tom scoffed, and that was the end of the matter as far as he was concerned.

During the time that Tom had been away from the office one of the other fellows had attended some revival meetings and had been converted. Now he urged Tom to come to one of the meetings with him. Since Tom had given up going to the pub, he found the evenings hard to occupy, and for want of something better to do he agreed.

They sat right at the back, where Tom could leave without making a disturbance if the going became too heavy; but the preacher, using a lot of verbal illustrations, made his topic interesting, and Tom listened to every word. At the end the speaker made a plea for the congregation to give their hearts to the Lord.

"Why don't you give your heart to the Lord, Tom?" his companion urged.

On the spur of the moment Tom could not think of any valid reason for refusing. He did not know exactly what "giving his heart to the Lord" entailed, but the preacher seemed to be a fine sort of chap and deeply in earnest, so Tom allowed himself to be piloted down the aisle, along with a lot of others who were "giving their hearts to the Lord." They went into a little back room, and after a while the preacher came down and prayed for them and shook hands with them and invited them all to come to church on Sunday, and that was the end of it. Tom did not feel any different; and he did not go back to the church on Sunday.

As the working days passed back at the office, Mrs. Prins kept nudging Tom about the meetings out at Claremont. "Have you been yet?" she would ask every few days. "It's quite close to where you live, Tom."

"No, I haven't been." He grinned at her. "Why should I go and listen to a bunch of false prophets?"

"Now, Tom, you're a fair man," she protested. "Why don't you go along and hear them before you form an opinion?"

Finally one Saturday night, when he had nothing else to do, Tom decided to surprise Mrs. Prins. He went along to the address she had given him and found the tent in darkness.

"I went," he gleefully informed Mrs. Prins on Monday morning, "but there wasn't any meeting. Nothing going on at all."

"Go again this week," she urged. "I know the lecture series hasn't finished yet."

111

Tom shrugged, but he went again the following Saturday night, and again the tent was dark and quiet.

"It's no use," he accosted Mrs. Prins on Monday. "Your prophets have flown. They're not having any meetings. Every time I go, the place is in darkness."

"Try once more," she insisted. "Go on a different night."

She was so sweet and so anxious for Tom to go and hear the evangelists that he agreed to try once more. Besides, she had told him that one of them was a singer named Turner, and he was curious to hear his "namesake" singing.

Tom went to the tent on Sunday night and found it ablaze with light and sound. The moment he stepped inside he knew that he was on the threshold of something different. The young fellows at the door shook hands heartily and handed him a program. A girl with the sweetest face he had ever seen ushered him to a seat. Soft music filled the air.

Tom settled into his seat and looked around. This was not what he had expected. This was so—so—— He could not put into words the tangible warmth of this atmosphere. The happiness and love radiating all around seemed like invisible arms reaching out to gather him in.

Presently a man stood up and began speaking. Tom did not know whether this was Turner or Hassenpflug, but whichever it was, he knew that what the man said was *truth*. The words rang in Tom's ears like the keen, clear tolling of bells on a still, cold night.

Monday night found him back at the tent. The fellows at the door were even more friendly, and the sweet-faced usherette smiled even more warmly. He went again on Tuesday. And on Wednesday. Tom attended every meeting until Saturday—and then he found that Saturday night was the only night that there was no meeting.

As time went by, Tom learned which evangelist was which. Harold Turner sang the gospel songs and Ben Hassenpflug did most of the preaching. Some of the subjects he expounded reminded Tom of what he had read in the lessons Mrs. Prins sent to him in the hospital.

The Taming of Thomas

Come to think of it, those lessons were not so bad. Tom went home and pulled them out of the bottom of his bag and checked them over again. His Bible was there too. He took it out and began reading it with fresh interest.

Tom continued attending the meetings every night. He urged Pat to come with him, but she refused. She attended her own church. "I don't want to get mixed up with any fly-by-night evangelists. Too many crazy religions originate in America." she said.

Tom stoutly defended his new friends, but Patricia was adamant, and gradually their friendship faded.

At the office Tom found it hard to concentrate on his work; questions popped into his head, and he had to have the answers immediately. Every moment they could spare found him and Mrs. Prins discussing the Bible.

Weeks passed. The evangelistic meetings drew to a close, and suddenly Tom discovered that all those loving, friendly people at the tent belonged to the Seventh-day Adventist Church. He was completely mystified. Presbyterians he knew, and Methodists and Baptists and Anglicans, but he had never heard of this religion before.

"Who are they?" he asked Mrs. Prins. "What does their name mean?"

"It means that they believe that Jesus Christ will return to earth soon—that's the Advent part; and they believe in obeying all the Ten Commandments. That's why they keep the seventh day, or Saturday, sacred."

Tom nodded. That made sense. He asked no more questions for a while. He needed time to think things over.

Before he could be baptized, the "Tent People," as Tom referred to his new friends, arranged for him to have Bible studies with Pastor Pike. Besides all the prophecies and Bible doctrines that he had heard in the lectures or read in the lessons, Tom now learned a more personal application of salvation. There were some things that he had to make right. The money he had stolen from the Deer's Hut till, for instance.

113

When Pastor Pike left after his final study, Tom reached for pen and paper. By dint of much frowning and memory prodding, he calculated the amount he had taken, added a generous 10 percent interest for all the intervening years, and posted the money with a letter of explanation to Mrs. White.

Her reply came by return post. "Dear Tom: Thank you for the money. I am so happy that you have become a Christian. You will never regret it. I see your father sometimes. He . . ."

After his baptism Tom joined the church nearest his lodgings in Claremont. A few weeks later, as he stood outside the church door with a group of young people, he was surprised by a hearty slap on his back and a familiar voice asking, "Tom, what are you doing here?"

Tom swung around. "Nurse George! What are *you* doing here?" They shook hands, and Tom said, "Are you one of them? Are you a Seventh-day Adventist too?"

George grinned. "Yes, I'm an 'Addie,' Tom. Say, there's someone else here that you'd know too. Hey, Bert."

A tall, lean young man detached himself from a group and came across to shake hands with Tom.

"I'm Bert Clifford, Tom. Do you remember me?"

Tom squinted at him. "Never saw you before."

Bert laughed. "Yes, you have, but I'm not surprised that you don't remember it. I know you because I was one of the medical students around your bed at Groote Schuur when our professor told us to diagnose which particular type of glandular fever you had."

Tom threw up his hands. "Sure is a small world."

The church members, young and old, welcomed Tom like a long-lost brother. They included him in all their church and social functions, and, settling into Seventh-day Adventist activities, he never felt lonely or missed his evenings spent at the pub with former friends.

As the weeks went by, Tom became more enthusiastic and more eager to work for the Lord. He decided to become a minister and preach the Word. Some of his new friends felt that Tom was not exactly ministerial material, and they tact-fully tried to direct him into other lines of service.

"You'd have to know Afrikaans before you could become a minister, Tom. That is the most common language here in South Africa. Why don't you try canvassing first? Selling religious books to the public is working for God."

"Yes," another friend chimed in. "It would take years of study for you to become a minister, Tom. But you could begin selling books right away."

"Fine, I'll do that." With his usual impulsiveness Tom accepted their advice. "But I'll study Afrikaans as well, so's I'll be ready. Do you know where I can find a tutor?

In a short time Tom resigned from his office job and began colporteur work. With his fluent tongue and ready wit he seemed amply equipped for success, but it did not come. He toiled for a whole year, watching his debts mount steadily month by month.

True, he sold some books, made a lot of interesting con-tacts, and saw one lady baptized as a direct result of his witnessing—but he had to eat. And he hated to be in debt. His Afrikaans lessons failed too. Despite his tutor's best efforts, Tom could not master the language.

"This can't be what the Lord wants me to do," Tom told the publishing department secretary. "There must be some other line of service for me."

But that worthy was not convinced. " 'No man having put his hand to the plough, and looking back, is fit for the king-dom of God,' " He quoted. "Pray about it before you make a decision, Tom."

Tom did pray about it, and a short time later he made a colossal sale, one that netted him over two thousand dollars commission. The publishing department secretary was jubi-lant. So was Tom—but for a different reason. He used the money to pay off his debts and went out and found himself a job with a paper manufacturing firm, E.S. and A. Robinson.

Back in an office doing slide-rule work as stock controller and estimator, Tom was happy. This was something he could handle. He would be content to serve his Lord as a layman.

Nearly two years rolled by, and then at a games social one Saturday night, Tom met Una Runkel. Nice girl, he thought, but the Seventh-day Adventist Church was full of nice girls. He'd already dated a few of them and found them refreshingly different from his former friends.

A few months later he visited the Goodwood church and saw Una again, and this time Cupid used his darts. Tom fell in love with Una, and she with him. They dated steadily for *two whole weeks* before announcing their engagement. Three months later, in October, 1956, they were married.

The young Turners set up housekeeping in a little cottage on the slopes of Helderberg Mountain, not far from the Seventh-day Adventist college. It was a lovely spot overlooking Tom's beloved ocean, with the mountain rising cold and clear behind them. Even on foggy, misty days when other peaks shrouded their heads in cloudy wraps, Helderberg Mountain stood out like a giant sentinel.

Five happy years passed. The little family doubled in size as first Linda-Jean and then her sister, Cheryl-Anne, arrived to delight their parents and grandparents.

The family attended the Strand church, where Tom was ordained first as a deacon and then as an elder. He enjoyed his church work; he enjoyed his daily work at Robinsons'; and he decided that this must be his niche. This was what the Lord wanted him to do, be a faithful witness where he was.

Then in 1962, not long after Tom's thirty-fifth birthday, the Lord spoke to him. The little family had recently returned from a holiday, and Tom was lying in bed recounting his blessings when he seemed to hear a voice say to him: "Why don't you study for the ministry now, Tom?"

"Study for the ministry? Now? Why, Lord, I'm thirty-five. I have a wife and two children to support. It just isn't possible now, Lord. I could have done it when I was younger and single, Lord—I wanted to then, but You didn't want me."

"I know all that. But I'm calling you *now*, Tom."

"But, Lord, there's still the little matter of learning Afrikaans."

"I know all about that too."

Like Moses at the burning bush, Tom found that he could not argue with the Lord. He told Una about his impression, and they talked it over and went to see Paster Van Eck, principal of Helderberg College.

Pastor Van Eck listened to their story, asked a few questions, and then said, "It's essential that you have your matriculation, Tom, and I don't think you'd be happy sitting in class with a lot of teenagers. Why don't you take private studies this year, sit for your matric; and if you pass, we'll enroll you in the theological course next year."

Tom nodded. That was sensible advice. No bridges burned. Nothing to lose if he failed—but if it was God's plan he knew he would not fail.

Other friends to whom he confided his plan reacted less optimistically. Most of them pointed out the insurmountable difficulties that faced a family man with as little educational background as Tom had. One well-meaning minister told him bluntly, "You're too old, Tom. God doesn't want old men in the ministry."

A few encouraged him. "It will be hard, Tom, don't make any mistake about that. But all things are possible with the Lord. If He wants you to become a minister, He will lead you."

Five days a week Tom worked a full eight hours for E.S. and A. Robinson, and at night he pored over his books and papers. It was nearly twenty years since he left school, and sometimes he found the facts and figures so hard to memorize that he wondered whether his brain had rusted.

But study was not Tom's only worry that year. First it was his feet. For weeks he limped around suffering the agonies of ingrowing toenails before he gave in and went to Dr. Mybrugh. The doctor examined his feet and nodded wisely.

"It's hospital for you, m'lad. You've pared and prodded at those toes until they're in a bad shape. We'll have to take the toenails off."

Tom grimaced, and the doctor said heartily, "Don't worry, we'll have you back on your feet in no time."

"I guess I'd better look on the bright side," Tom said when he told Una the bad news. "I can take my books to the hospital with me and get in a few days of concentrated study."

Only a matter of months later Tom developed a cold and a sore throat that refused to respond to gargles or compresses or any other home remedies that solicitous friends and relatives suggested. In the end Una insisted he see the doctor.

When Tom painfully croaked out his symptoms, that same jovial doctor adjusted his little spotlight, peered into Tom's inflamed throat, and cheerfully announced: "Your tonsils are in a bad way, young man. I'll give you something to clear up the inflammation, and then you'll have to go into the hospital for a tonsillectomy. Don't worry, it doesn't hurt—much."

Tom was still savoring the delight of swallowing solid food without wincing when his third physical misfortune struck.

Sitting at his desk in midafternoon, busily working out a series of complicated costing figures, he presently became aware of a nagging pain in his right side.

He tried to ignore the sensation and go on with his work, but the pain refused to be ignored. It grew worse and worse. By the time Tom staggered home that evening he was retching and groaning in agony.

The doctor looked grave as he poked and prodded Tom's abdomen. It's an appendectomy and a week or so in the hospital for you, young fellow."

"Oh, no, not now," Tom groaned. "It's only a month or two until exams."

But Dr. Myburgh insisted. "Yes, right now. Just as soon as I can arrange a bed for you."

Finally the long year dragged to its painful close. Tom sat for his examinations, and to his delight, and the astonishment of others, he passed.

Pastor Van Eck kept his word, and at the beginning of the 1963 college year Tom moved his family onto the Helderberg campus. With 100 pounds (280 dollars) in his pocket and faith in his heart, he commenced the four-year training course.

Tom thought 1962 had been a hard year, but it was a bed of roses compared with what he was up against now. Every day except Sabbath he worked and studied and worked some more. He swept the library. He drew up building plans for his father-in-law's business. He did any job that came his way, and more besides. Midnight found him still nodding over his books, and at 4:00 AM he was up again to take a physical training class.

But despite his best efforts, as the months passed, Tom's debts mounted steadily—and his grades declined equally as steadily.

Tom hit rock bottom the day the professor returned the psychology test papers. He turned to the last page and stared at the red figures—4/15. Surely that could not be correct. He'd tried so hard.

"It's no use, Lord," he groaned inaudibly. "I can't do it. It's harder than I thought, and I'm too tired to study. I'm too tired to work. I wish I could go away somewhere and sleep for a month."

When Una conveyed the news of Tom's discouragement to her parents, those kindhearted people talked it over and came up with a face-saving idea.

"Look here, Tom," Mr. Runkel suggested. "Instead of all this bother of my working out the value of each job you do for me and paying you accordingly, why don't I pay you a regular weekly wage and you just do all of my building plans for me?"

Tom gratefully accepted the suggestion, but the salary was still insufficient for all their needs. Then Una was offered a job assisting in the college store. This was something she could handle while keeping an eye on her two preschoolers playing under the trees outside the store. Her small salary was a welcome addition to their meager funds, and they praised the Lord for it, but it did not eliminate all worries. There were still expensive textbooks to purchase, laboratory fees, and clothing replacements for little girls who seemed to grow like weeds.

Tom and Una practiced every economy they had ever heard or read about, but the struggle was unequal. Things would go along fine for a while, and then some unexpected, unbudgeted-for expense would crop up, and worry lines creased Tom's forehead.

Did God want old men in the ministry? Doubts crowded in, and the future looked like an impossible dream. Then Tom thought of his past life. His faith strengthened, and he prayed all the harder. There was a reason for it, just as Mac said in Trieste so long ago. God had called him. God would provide.

"Look at this!" Tom's usual optimism bubbled above his worries as he bounded into the house, waving a letter from the Southern African Division. "It says here that they've granted me a bursary of 250 pounds (700 dollars) for my first two college years. That will help with my fees, and I'll be able to spend a little more time in study. Isn't the Lord good?" He grabbed Una in an impulsive bear hug.

Daddy, Daddy," Linda-Jean and Cheryl-Anne shrilled as they left their play and rushed at him. Grabbing a leg each and hugging it tightly, they clamored to be picked up and jigged around in boisterous Daddy-fashion.

All of these unexpected windfalls eased their financial burdens tremendously, but the Lord had not finished bestowing His blessings. In September of that year Tom received a letter from England. The envelope boasted a big blob of red sealing wax, and Tom guessed that it contained important news. He had no idea what it could be and rushed into the kitchen where Una was scrubbing vegetables for supper.

"Here's a letter from Liphook."

"From your father?"

"No. He hardly ever writes."

Una stopped scrubbing and listened while Tom read the letter aloud, interpreting the legal terms as he went along. " . . . from the estate of the late deceased . . . until the whereabouts of the second issue . . . the last will and testament . . ."

He read it again, and they stared at each other open-mouthed, scarcely comprehending. Then Tom said, "All of which seems to mean that poor ŏld Dad died last December and they couldn't find me until now. George must've come across one of my old letters in Dad's things."

He swallowed hard and was silent a moment before adding, "But the part of the solicitor's letter that concerns us now is that when Dad's estate is settled we'll get 2,500 pounds (7,000 dollars)."

"Two thousand five hundred pounds!" Una gasped out the words. "Why, that's a small fortune."

"It is to us," Tom agreed. He took Una's grocery order pad from the wall and began scribbled calculations. After a few minutes of frowning and figuring he looked up: "Well, liefling,* the Lord has done it again. If everything remains as it is now, with both of us working our hardest and no unexpectedly large expenses, that money will see us through to graduation. Of course we'll have a tight budget and I'll have to canvass for all I'm worth during vacations, but at least we won't have a mountain of debts looming in front of us all the way.

Una nodded. She was too close to tears to reply.

In October, 1966, no graduates felt happier than Tom and Una Turner. During the past work-filled four years Una had had no time to take regular college studies, but Tom insisted that she was a graduate too. "If I've earned my BA in Theology," he told his friends, "then Una deserves a PhT for Putting Hubby Through."

When all the excitement of that glorious, victorious, blessed day died down, Tom had a decision to make.

"God doesn't want old men in the ministry, Tom," the well-meaning minister had told him before he began his course. Now at its close, five conferences from Uganda to the Cape, called for his services. In his usual way Tom turned to the Lord for guidance and was impressed to accept the call to

---

*Afrikaans for "lovey."

pastor two churches at Port Elizabeth.

A short vacation by the sea blew all the tiredness and tenseness away, and an exuberant Turner family proceeded to the new post at Port Elizabeth.

Tom's enthusiasm subsided a little when he learned that the Port Elizabeth church had a large percentage of Afrikaans-speaking members and he would be expected to preach in Afrikaans every second Sabbath. Besides that, the second church, at Uitenhage, was composed entirely of Afrikaans-speaking members and every sermon delivered there had to be in Afrikaans.

"I hadn't thought of that," he groaned to Una. "Good thing we had to preach one sermon in Afrikaans in order to graduate. At least that's one sermon I have ready."

"Good thing you have an Afrikaans-speaking wife, too," Una reminded him.

So Tom commenced his ministry. Each week he wrote out a new sermon, and Una pored over it for hours, faithfully translating each word into Afrikaans. Then Tom asked one of the church members who spoke fluent Afrikaans and English to go over the sermon with him and correct the idioms, coach him in pronouncing difficult words, and generally polish up the presentation. When that was done he read it over at least ten times, so that by the time the sun set on Friday he could almost deliver the sermon from memory.

Week after week Tom followed that program, sandwiched in between his multitudinous other tasks of visiting and counseling. When he stepped down from the pulpit at noon on Sabbath mornings his sweat-soaked shirt told its tale, but not once did he have to resort to preaching an English sermon in an Afrikaans service.

It would take another book to record Tom's adventures as he worked for the Lord in various parts of South Africa. However, it will be sufficient to say here that in 1974, after much prayer and a series of providential promptings, Tom and Una, with their two daughters and seven-year old son,

The Taming of Thomas

Jimmy, arrived in Australia to continue their ministerial work for the Lord.

Looking back over his life, Tom sees God's hand protecting him through all his wild escapades and numerous narrow escapes. He regrets the years he squandered in foolish indifference to God's claims, and he tells his life story here in the sincere hope that it may serve to help young people everywhere to "remember now thy Creator in the days of thy youth" (Ecclesiastes 12:1).

Fascinating nature adventure . . .

A Mink's Story
by Emil Liers

Spotting Alusa, "the dark one," far below, the Cooper's hawk hurtled toward her. Unaware of her danger, Alusa slipped under some bent wild rice stalks, and the frustrated hawk slashed through the air toward her.

For a moment the hawk hovered overhead, and Alusa, at last spotting him, screamed defiance at the predator. Then the hawk crash-dived into the massed stalks, trying to reach the mink. Angry that she had eluded him, he forced his talons through the rice stalks. As he reached for her, Alusa bit his leg, grasping one of the leg joints.

The fierce hawk now closed his talons and beat his wings as he tried to lift Alusa clear of the vegetation so he could kill her with his beak. Alusa still clung to his leg. The talons on the other leg had involuntarily closed on some tough rice stalks. With a scream, the hawk struggled to pull free. Mice had dug among the roots. The roots began to loosen in the soil. Realizing that the stalks were pulling out of the ground, he beat his wings harder and slowly rose into the air while the mink gnawed more determinedly at his leg.

Experience the exciting adventure for survival that Alusa and her mink kittens live every day in A MINK'S STORY. Available at your nearest Adventist Book Center for only US$1.95. Or use the handy order form found in the back of this book.

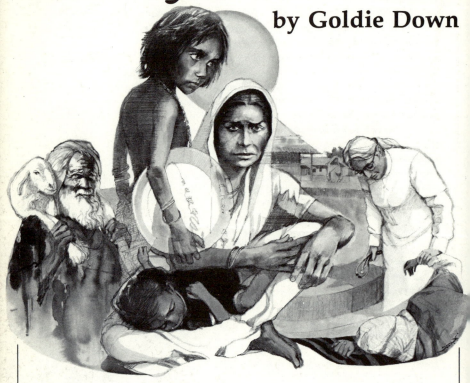

ORDER BLANK

Qty.	Title	Price Each*	Total
	Adventure at Beaver Falls	$4.50	
	Demon of Padeng	5.95	
	No Forty-Hour Week	4.50	
	A Mink's Story	1.95	
	Subtotal		
	Sales tax for your state		
	Postage & handling 10 percent of subtotal (minimum 75¢)		
	Total (amount enclosed)		

*Prices in U.S. dollars

Send along with check or money order to:

ABC Mailing Service

Box 37485

Omaha, NE 61837

or

ABC Mailing Service

Box 398

Oshawa, Ontario L1H 7L5

_____

(your name)

_____

(address)

_____

(city)   (state)   (zip)